MY AMERICA

A BABY-BOOMER MEMOIR LIVING UNDER PRESIDENTS TRUMAN TO BIDEN

By Roger Carter

CONTENTS

Introduction

In the 75+ years that I have been around, I have seen, heard, and read a lot of things about our country. There have been times when it seemed that we were making progress improving the lives of our citizens and there have been times when we seemed to be stepping back. I have tried to put to ink my honest opinions of all the Presidents during my lifetime and how I think their administrations affected me and the country. I have seen how we can work together and become a stronger, better nation and I have seen what happens when we don't try and live up to our stated values. I think we may be facing some dangers to our democracy, but I do believe that we the people can overcome them. I don't expect everyone to agree with me and that is your right. However, I hope these words I've written might make you stop and think about what it really is to be a citizen and a patriot. Thank you for reading my memoir.

Roger Carter

"First they came for the socialist, and I did not speak out – because I was not a socialist. Then they came for the trade unionists, and I did not speak out – because I was not a trade unionist. Then they came for the Jews, and I did not speak out – because I was not a Jew. Then they came for me – and there was no one left to speak for me." - Pastor Martin Niemoller

CHAPTER 1

The Shaping of My Thoughts and Believes

I am proud to be an American. I am fortunate to have been born in a democracy with a republican form of government that has allowed me to live and experience many things. We have our problems just like other countries but I think we have always tried to do what we believe is right. There have been times though when what we thought was right, well maybe it wasn't.

We are a very diverse nation. We are many races, religions, ethnic groups, and immigrants come from every nation in the world. We struggle daily to live up to our beliefs of being a free people, a nation that puts the individual rights ahead of all else. Sometimes though we fail.

As I start this Joe Biden has become President of the United States and former President Trump was impeached for a second time, only this time for insurrection against the government, and the Senate failed again to convict based on Party lines predominantly and not achieving the 2/3 majority needed for conviction. This happened even though Republican members of both houses, and the Vice-President of the United States and our very democracy were targets of the insurrection. They initially spoke out against what happened and then they changed their tune. Why? What happened? Maybe by the time I get to the end of this we will have some answers.

January 6, 2021 a mob of extremist attacked the Capitol in an attempt to stop the certification of the electoral votes making Joe Biden President of the United States and overturn the results of the election keeping Donald Trump in office. This was a planned operation by armed radical groups of militias, including the Proud Boys, Oath Keepers, the Three Percenters, neo-Nazi hate groups, the KKK, and Q-Anon conspiracy believers. This was announced in advance, months before it occurred, hinted at by President Trump and others, yet no one was paying attention or taking it seriously. How could this happen? It wasn't a surprise to me.

We are in the middle of a pandemic unlike anything seen in over 100 years. It has killed over 1 million Americans and infected millions of others. How has this happened? Why are there so many people that still believe that this is a false flag, something cooked up by the government and the Democrats? What in the world is going on America?

When I was born the country was different. We only had 48 states. It would be 1959 during the Eisenhower administration before Alaska and Hawaii would become states. America today is different in many ways culturally than what I grew up in but at the same time there are many similarities. I think we are experiencing the repercussions of ignoring not only what we should know historically of our country, but what we have lived through since World War II and how my generation was raised. We have to recognize and understand our past to move into the future.

The parents of many of us "Baby-Boomers" grew up in a different world than we did. They lived through World War I, a pandemic, the great depression and personally knew poverty, food shortages, discrimination, and fought in their own major world war. Their parents may have fought in WWI or the Spanish-American war and their grandparents had probably fought in the Civil War. All of those family experiences added to my life and way of thinking. I understand how that can give anyone a different outlook on life.

Many of our parents weren't very well educated. I knew a lot of people as a child who could neither read nor write, or their skills were very limited. My father had only a second grade education because it was believed he was needed more on the farm to work than waste time going to school. Most Americans of his generation didn't know much about the world other than their local communities. Many still didn't have electricity or running water.

America was still climbing out of our own problems as the world was contenting with Nazism, Fascists, Communists, and dictators. When World War II came to our doorstep Americans were forced into changes that they were not prepared for. Great sacrifices were made by all the families across the country no matter what class, race, ethnic, or religious background they came from. With the manpower demands of the war, women took on jobs in industry doing work that before was only done by men. The economy was all based on supporting the war effort.

When the war ended veterans came home to a new America. The trauma that many had experienced would live with them forever and determine how they looked at the world. They wanted to put the war behind them but they still had challenges ahead of them. The country was changing from a wartime economy to a peacetime economy. There were housing shortages, material shortages, lack of automobiles, and other domestic needs. There was also a large influx of new people, immigrants from war torn parts of the world coming to America and competing for the good life that everyone wanted. Minority Americans, especially the two million black veterans, wanted an equal chance and their rights as American citizens respected. Change was coming along with the competition for a better life and we had a new enemy, Communism.

I don't have all the answers but I have lived through and have seen a real change in my country, some good and some bad. This is about my America and my story growing up as a Baby-Boomer.

As I write this I am a 75 year old, white male, retired military veteran that served in the US Navy and US Air Force. Politically I am a centrist conservative with conventional views, fiscal conservative, social moderate, believe in a strong defense, free but fair trade, protecting the environment, legal immigration, limited government, but bi-partisan government. I came from a family of Democrats and until recently I was a lifelong Republican. I was born December 1946 in Owensboro, Kentucky. My family was middle-class or lower-middle class would be more accurate. My mother worked as a waitress, cleaned rooms at a hotel and my dad, a WWII Navy veteran, worked labor jobs in a wagon wheel factory in Owensboro. I had 2 half-sisters and a half-brother. Eventually the family moved to Lake County, Indiana where the steel mills, better paying jobs, and manufacturing was picking up.

My earliest memory of my mother was when she was dying of cancer and wanted to return home to Kentucky. Mom moved us and we were living at my grandparents' home in Livermore, KY. My father was still working in Indiana. There was a housing shortage and wages were pretty low compared to today. The federal minimum wage was 40 cents an hour.

A TIME OF ROCKWELL AMERICANA

Following the death of my mother just weeks before my 4th birthday, I lived with my grandparents for a year. I followed my "Pappy Joe" (grandfather) around like a little puppy dog.

We lived in a house that had no electricity. Grandma cooked on a wood burning stove and washed clothes in an outside kettle over a fire. We had an outhouse for the toilet, and heated the home with fireplaces. Not everyone had cars and I saw a lot of horses and wagons used.

My grandfather, a WWI veteran, had been Mayor of Livermore at one time and he knew everyone. Livermore was a small town on the Green River and Rough River junction with a railroad bridge that mechanically turned over the river to let boats and barges through, a daily bus stop, a ferry (operated by my uncle) that carried cars, wagons, and people across the river, and a bridge built by the WPA during the depression years.

The town itself had a town square where most of the businesses were located and a National Guard armory. It was a prosperous town laid out in 1837. Most of the homes were modest but there were several that looked like mansions of the Old South. Population if my memory serves me right, was approximately 1200 people. Everyone was so friendly and as a young child I never was scared of anyone or anything.

My day generally started with a hot bath (water heated on the wood cook stove) and a great breakfast cooked by grandma. Clean freshly ironed clothes were mandatory wear (iron was heated on the stove), and I must have had to change clothes at least twice a day. Appearance was important even if you didn't have much. I always felt sorry for grandma since she had a hunch back, was hard of hearing, wore glasses, and yet took such good care of all of us living there. When she wasn't busy I would sit on the porch with her in a rocking chair until Pappy Joe was ready for our daily trips.

Every day we would take the short walk into town with the first stop being the tractor store. There Pappy Joe would talk with his friends and I would play with the model tractors they had in their window. I don't remember anyone ever smoking at these gatherings but they sure chewed tobacco. Spittoons were common at all houses and businesses. I thought I was a big guy and tried some tobacco chewing there one time and learned that I never wanted to do that again!

Leaving the tractor store we generally walked over to the Post Office. The bus stop was near there and that's how I remember the mail being brought into town. It seemed like everyone in town was there for their mail. We then would sometimes go to a furniture factory nearby and visit for a while before resuming our journey.

Crossing the street to the main square we must have stopped at every store in town. The stores weren't like big name stores you see today but small "General Stores" where you could buy almost anything. We never missed stopping in one of the stores and talking with the people working there.

Next we would go to the National Guard armory. They had tanks there which I thought was a really big deal. Heading around the town square corner we would walk to several restaurant locations many of which were closed. One in particular got my attention because the concrete sidewalk had a ton of marbles in the concrete. I found out that my mother at one time had worked there and she was the one that had put the marbles in the concrete.

We generally went on to the drug store which had a counter where you could by sodas and ice-cream. Our next stop would be at the Town Marshall's office. He and Pappy Joe were real good friends. I remember the Marshall showed me all of his guns and he let me hold them.

The rest of the morning we would walk down to the river where the ferry crossing was located. One of my uncles operated the ferry. Vehicles and passengers would be taken across the river. I got to ride one time. Generally, we would just sit and watch the river traffic. Once I saw what I thought was a Navy ship, but I was told that it was the Coast Guard patrolling the river.

Life was pretty simple. Radio (if you had electricity), and world news clips at the movie house, and reading the paper was how you got the news. Televisions were virtually non-existent at the time and we certainly didn't have anything like computers!

Normally for evening entertainment Pappy Joe or an uncle would give me a quarter and I would go to the movie house. I thought I was walking by myself but Pappy Joe was actually following me. With the quarter I could get into the movie and be able to buy a coke and popcorn. Most of the movies that I remember were westerns with Roy Rogers, Gene Autry, or some other famous cowboy star. You always knew who the good guys were because they wore white hats and the bad guys wore black hats (symbolic of something?).

They also showed serials like the Range Rider or Flash Gordon.

Sometimes there were other things to do. Once there was a travelling skating ring that came to town. They would put up a tent and flooring and my sister and her friends went roller skating. But times were changing. One of the General Stores had a big window and sitting in it was a television. Sometimes at night they would turn that television on. They had speakers hanging outside and there would be a small crowd of people standing around on the sidewalk watching it.

Another thing I remember is that I only saw two people that looked different than anyone else, a black man that delivered papers and a black man that drove a horse and wagon that delivered fire wood. I never saw a kid that looked different than me. Real Rockwell Americana.

CHANGING TIMES

My first real memory of my dad was when he came and moved me and my two sisters, back to Lake County, Indiana. Life was changing. East Chicago was where we lived, a big city at the time. People were everywhere. Nothing like Livermore.

Steel mills, oil refineries, all kinds of industry were there rebuilding America.

We lived in a 2nd floor, one bedroom apartment above Ralph's bar. The building was made of wood except the front of the bar. There was a housing shortage and it was tough to find a place to live. Our local grocery store (Joe's) was a little mom and pop operation owned by a couple that spoke funny. They had some kind of accent that I had never heard before. I didn't know at the time, but there were a lot of people living in East Chicago with an accent.

Following the conclusion of World War II, many people immigrated to the US. Whereas we were called "Hillbillies" because we moved up from Kentucky, these people were referred to as "DPs", displaced persons. Italians were "Whops or Dagos". Polish people were "Dumb Pollock's". Mexicans were "Wetbacks", Germans were "Krauts", and Black Americans were the N-word. I am sure there were some other nasty names used for other people.

Listening to adults talk I knew they didn't really like these people for they felt they were taking jobs away from them or just plain prejudice fed by ignorance, and some came from countries we had just defeated in the war. There were neighbors from Greece, Poland, Germany, Hungary, and other European countries. Many of them lived in little neighborhoods that consisted strictly of people from the old country. Missing in our neighborhood were Orientals and Blacks.

My dad hated the Japanese. I like to think this was because he had fought in the Pacific and they were the enemy he had to face. He didn't speak much about the war but when he did he had nothing good to say about the Japanese people.

Many of the movies at the time were about WWII. As a child I thought we were still at war with them.

I am sure how I look at the world and our country today is a result of my upbringing, education, politics at various times, along with my real life experiences as an adult.

So far there have been 14 presidents during my lifetime. I am going to address some of what happened during their presidencies and how it affected me at the time and how it affects my and I believe many other baby-boomers outlook on today. It's important to note that a president is supposed to be limited in power. Their successes and failures have a lot to do with which party held power in congress and who was on the Supreme Court at the time of their presidency.

CHAPTER 2

Harry S. Truman, Democrat, April 12, 1945 – January 1953

Researching the National Archives and the Harry S. Truman Library I found information of what was going on during his presidency, since I was too little to know, but it would affect me and other baby boomers for the rest of our lives. The month I was born was when Truman signed the proclamation declaring the end of hostilities for World War II.

It was 1946 when I was born, the Democrats controlled both houses of congress and Harry S. Truman was President. Truman was a WWI veteran, a captain in field artillery. He became President with the death of Franklin D. Roosevelt in 1945 and led the country through the end of WWII and the start of the Korean War until January 1953. It was Truman that authorized the atomic bombing of Japan and brought the war to an end. America was militarily strong (we were the only country with the bomb) but tired of war. Unfortunately a new enemy came to the forefront, communism.

In 1946 the Union of Soviet Socialist Republics (USSR/Russia today) controlled most of Eastern Europe and occupied those countries and half of

Germany by the close of WWII. The USSR under the firm hand of Stalin had bigger plans though. Stalin and the Communists wanted to control the world and it really was only the United States that stood in their way (after all we had the bomb and our infrastructure hadn't been attacked during the war).

Truman took action with the backing of the Republicans in congress and appropriated money to fight the spread of communism in Greece and Turkey. This was known as the Truman Doctrine. He also ordered loyalty investigations of all federal employees. He signed the National Security Act that unified the armed forces under one department, the Department of Defense, the US Air Force (from which I retired) and established the CIA and National Security Council, all of which still exists today. The Republicans took control of both houses in 1947 to 1949.

In 1948 Truman asked congress for civil rights legislation to secure the rights of the country's minority groups. Something that the minority veterans wanted. That didn't get too far. Even though his party won back control of both houses 1949 to 1953, the final six years of his presidency, the Southern Democrats opposed any racial integration or expansion of civil rights for Black Americans and other minorities. They were so opposed that they formed the States Rights Party usually called Dixiecrats, to oppose Truman's re-election. Their candidate was Senator Strom Thurman, an extreme segregationist.

Truman would eventually have to desegregate the armed forces by executive order. Later that year when Truman won the Democratic nomination, 35 delegates from Alabama and Mississippi walked out of the convention in protest of a strong civil rights plank in the party platform. He also signed the Displaced Persons Act which authorized admission of over 205,000 Europeans over a two year period.

A DANGEROUS WORLD

If things weren't challenging enough on the home front, the Russians blockaded that portion of Berlin controlled by the West. NATO and Soviet forces faced each other with tanks. It was a real hair-trigger situation. Truman ordered the Berlin Airlift flying food and coal into West Berlin, which lasted almost a full year before the Russians backed down.

I mentioned earlier that there was a housing shortage following WWII. In 1949 Truman signed the Housing Act, a national housing policy that provided federal aid to low cost housing projects and slum removal programs. Things were picking up. Most of those homes were two bedroom houses around 900 square foot. As a kid I lived in a few of those.

September of 1949 something else that would affect my life and the world occurred. Russia exploded their first Atomic bomb! Four months later Truman ordered the development of the Hydrogen bomb. Life was about to change again.

On June 25th, 1950 the North Korean army attacked the South. American troops were already there and took a beating at the beginning of the war and were driven to a small enclave in South Korean. Under the leadership of General MacArthur the North Koreans were beaten back by November and the US and UN troops were in North Korea up to the Chinese border. It looked like the war would soon be over, but then the Chinese army came to North Korea's aid. Overwhelmed, UN forces were driven back south again. The North Koreans were also receiving assistance from the Union of Soviet Socialist Republics (USSR or Russia as known today). Both China and the USSR had been our allies during WWII against Japan, Italy, and Germany.

This conflict wasn't called a war but a "policing action" under the United Nations leadership. Also in November there was an assassination attempt by two Puerto Rican nationalist against Truman, not a good month for the President.

Many people thought we should use atomic weapons in Korea to stop the Chinese, but in 1949 the Soviet Union had exploded their first atomic weapon. The United States was no longer the sole power with these terrible weapons. Tensions were growing between the U.S. and the Soviet Union. The cold war was on and there was fear that atomic weapons would be the end of everybody if it went from cold to hot between our two countries.

ON THE HOME FRONT

In March of 1952 Truman announced that he wasn't running for re-election. Three months later construction began on the USS Nautilus, the world's first atomic powered submarine.

At home things were looking up. As a union man, Dad's work was finally pretty steady and he was making enough money that we had a used car, a party-line telephone, and finally our own television set. We still listened to the radio primarily because television was still a relatively new thing with limited programming and hours of operation. On the radio they had programs like the Lone Ranger, The Range Rider, The Shadow, Gang Busters, and comedy shows like Amos and Andy, and Jack Benny. All these programs would eventually become well known television shows in the early years of broadcasting.

Our news still came primarily from reading newspapers, radio, some television (maybe twice a day for half an hour of local then national news), and news of the world at the movie houses.

My dad had married again to a woman whose family had come from old Europe. I believe they were Hungarian. I was old enough to start school and a whole new world opened up to me. One of the first things I had to learn was the Pledge of Allegiance. Every school day started like that until I graduated from high school. This simple little thing instilled a pride in my country and the importance of being an American that is still with me today.

Until school I didn't have very many kids my age to play with. It was in school that I made friends with a young boy named Nelson. We were best buddies. His family had moved here from Puerto Rico and they were fantastic people. I don't know what his dad did to make a living, but his father was a great magician and his mother a great cook. Nelson and I spent a lot of time together going to the park or visiting each other's house. His family treated me like I was one of their kids. Unfortunately when we moved away from East Chicago I never saw my friend again.

Something else important happened in 1952, the first televised political convention. Both parties held their convention in Chicago. The Republican convention was first and Five-Star General Dwight D. Eisenhower was their candidate with Richard Nixon as the Vice-President candidate. The Democratic Party selected Adlai Stevenson. The conventions were covered by all three stations, CBS, ABC, and NBC.

We watched and I was fascinated by what the people were doing, carrying signs, yelling, bands playing, and different people giving speeches. Dad had to explain to me what it was all about, but it sure looked like fun. I remember asking who he was going to vote for and he said the Democrats. When I asked him why he said because the Republican

Party was for the rich people and the Democratic Party for the working man.

Out of curiosity while writing this, I looked up on Wikipedia what the Republican platform was in 1952. Here's what I found:

1. End the war in Korea
2. Use nukes as a deterrence to the USSR
3. Keep the Taft-Hartley Act (this would restrict the activities and power of the Unions (I give that one to you dad)
4. Oppose discrimination
5. Eliminate lynching
6. End Communist subversion in the US.

Eisenhower won the election. Sorry dad.

My opinion: Truman is quoted and remembered for his statement, "The Buck Stops Here". That taught me that when you are the person making decisions, good or bad, you as a leader accept the responsibility for the results of that decision. You don't pass the blame onto others for your failures. Maybe some leaders today need to learn and remember that.

CHAPTER 3

Dwight D. Eisenhower, GOP, January 1953 – January 1961

Eisenhower (more often referred to as IKE) became the 34th President. The Republican Party also won control of both the House and Senate, which would only last until 1955. They would never control either the House or the Senate again until 1981. I started first grade with Ike's election and he would remain my President until my final year of Junior High.

We still moved a lot. By the time Ike finished his two terms, I had attended six different grade schools and two different junior high schools. Talk about getting a diverse education!

GRADE SCHOOL YEARS

I enjoyed school and had great teachers. Most of them were women and they really helped me grow. You see, my stepmother wasn't the nicest person in the world and so it was enriching to have women that inspired and motivated me to want to learn. I had some problems at first and it was my teacher that realized I couldn't see what was written on the blackboard. She moved me to the front of the class and called my parents in and told them to get me some glasses.

Going to grade school at that time was rather different than today. The events of the world brought a different light to learning. We were taught not only reading, writing, and arithmetic, but also how to **duck and cover in case an atomic bomb** was dropped on us. This was very real. The Cold War was always on the verge of becoming a Hot War. Living in Lake County Indiana just southeast of Chicago, Illinois, and being the heart of the steel industry, and other manufacturing, made us a prime target if war broke out between the US and the USSR.

The Korean War was brought to an end by President Eisenhower. He convinced the American people, South Korea, and China that a negotiated peace was better than the consequences of failing to reach an agreement. An armistice was negotiated and remains in effect to this day.

Now we had only one major international enemy and it was the USSR. The Russians had bombers that could reach the Continental US. To combat that possibility we had air-to-ground missile sites around major cities and industrial areas. One was located near where we lived and if you drove from Dyer, IN to Munster, IN (maybe 10 miles) you drove right by an active Nike missile site. We moved from Dyer to Munster.

Munster was a small town, maybe 5,000 people, located just south of Hammond, IN. Nice community. Most of the homes were nicer than the place we rented. The school I attended was rather small but within walking distance for me. I wasn't there long, but I do remember that all the students were white.

In 1953 Joseph Stalin the ruler of the USSR died. The world gave a sigh of relieve. He was replaced by Nikita Khrushchev, who would remain in power until 1964. He was considered more liberal, but still a very dangerous adversary. I didn't feel any safer in school and doubted that I would ever live to become an adult. On top of all this the US and USSR were conducting above ground testing of nuclear and hydrogen bombs. **I wonder where all that fallout went**?

We moved again, this time to Black Oak, IN. It was an unincorporated area near Gary, IN. The only way I can describe it is that it was swampy wet land. It was a little bit of country living and had the biggest mosquitos in the world. The house we lived in had a long front yard where we planted a garden. We had a few neighbors including some Polish immigrants that lived in a basement type house. I thought they were nice people, but others just called them "Dumb Pollock". When I started elementary school there, I finally saw kids that looked different than me. I didn't think anything about it, but they lived in a different part of Black Oak then we did. Consequently I only knew them from school. That was the first time I had ever heard the N-word used by anyone my age.

For some reason I had to go to another school in the township for a little while. I had a great teacher that taught us everything including science, geography, and history. Indiana history was mandatory and I really loved it. We also received a small paper every week called the Weekly Reader. It had stories related to what we were being taught in class. I remember one story about the ice at the North and South poles. The scientist were predicting that by the year 2000 the poles would be melting. **(Global warming?)**

One day in class we were studying geography and had a world map hanging on the wall. I was really staring at it and my teacher asked what was I looking so hard at. I told her that it looked like a jigsaw puzzle. She asked me what I meant and I said it looked to me like you could almost move the continents around and they would fit together. Later that week she had a friend that was a professor at Indiana University stop by. Introducing me to the professor I was asked to tell her what I had told my teacher. After I did, she asked how I thought the continents ended up like they are now. My answer was they float on the water **(continental drift?)** So much for becoming a famous scientist.

HATE AND FEAR AT HOME

While my simple life was going on there was a Republican senator from Wisconsin named Joe McCarthy that was accusing people of being members of the communist party. He played on the fear of the American people. He made many serious charges against government employees, movie stars, people in the news media, members of the military, and others and didn't have any proof of the charges he made. The lives of many people were ruined. It wasn't until someone stood up to him in a senate hearing that he finally stood down. Almost sounds like some politicians of today. He left the Senate in 1957 in disgrace.

In 1953 Ike signed the Refugee Relief Act which allowed 214,000 more European immigrants to the US than under the then visa quota system. During this same time "Operation Wetback" (yes that was the real name) began and deported 1.3 million undocumented illegal Mexicans from California, Arizona, and Texas. Despite statements to the contrary, this was not done with US troops but it was ordered by the President. What it did do was disrupt agricultural work in those areas. **Sound familiar?**

In 1954 the Supreme Court abolished segregation in public schools. There was tremendous objection throughout the country which was about 90% white, but mainly in the southern states the Democrats (Dixiecrats) didn't support anything that might uplift Black Americans who were being discriminated against. The policy up until then was separate but equal schools.

By 1955 I had started 3rd grade and was paying more attention to what was on the evening news. News programs weren't 24/7 as they are today. We had half an hour of local and half an hour of national news may be twice a day.

August of that year a young boy named Emmett Till was murdered in Mississippi for allegedly flirting with a white woman. His killers were acquitted. I saw the pictures of his body.

Then there was a woman in Montgomery, AL that had caused quite a stir. Her name was Rosa Parks. Apparently she had taken a seat on a bus that was for white people and she wouldn't give it up. I had never known of such a thing as seats only for white people. That sure sounded dumb. I learned that was the law in many states especially in the South. Schools, water fountains, waiting areas at bus stations, and restaurants had separate areas for whites and for blacks. Someone forgot to tell the South and some of the Northern cities about the 14th Amendment to the Constitution.

The mid-50s was the start of the civil rights movement as I grew to know it because of the aggression and murders going on by the Ku Klux Klan and state governments' efforts to prevent Black and Brown US Citizens from exercising their rights.

In 1956 the Eisenhower's Federal Aid Highway Act was passed. This was the start of the Interstate Highway system. I was able to watch the interstate being built right in front of the home we lived in. It was very impressive and made you feel proud to be an American.

At the same time, in Hungary the people revolted against the Soviets. Tanks were in the streets of Budapest and the rebellion was put down by the Communists. Over 38,000 educated Hungarian refugees came to America as a result of the revolt. We watched the revolt on the evening news.

1957 was a tough year for the country. Eisenhower sponsored and signed the Civil Rights Bill of 1957 but Congress, mainly the Southern Democrats, weakened it.

To make matters worse, the USSR launched the first ICBM (Intercontinental Ballistic Missile) in May, capable of carrying a nuclear warhead and deployed it in 1958. We didn't have that capability and didn't have one to deploy until 1959. Oh, by the way Nike missiles couldn't shoot an ICBM down.

In October 1957 the Soviets launched Sputnik. The country was in a panic. What was that thing anyway? Did it have some type of bomb on it? Am I ever going to live to adulthood?

We had a problem in Little Rock Arkansas when their governor sent National Guard troops to keep 9 black students from attending Central High School. The president ended up having to send elements of the 101st Airborne to protect the students from potential rioters. The military is needed to go to school?

As for me school was going fine. Of course we had moved a couple of more times and I had to switch schools again. It was around 5th or 6th grade (1958 or 1959) that I had a male teacher. He was really good and was a veteran from either WWII or Korea. I'm not sure which, but he made history class really interesting.

He was like a hero to all the boys in class and played ball with us during recess periods. One day a bunch of us guys were just talking with him and the question came up as to whether he thought we boys would ever go to war like he had. I remember his answer as clear as day, "I guarantee it. Hitler once said that the world needed a war every 15yrs just to keep the people in check". That was thought provoking considering the state of the world at that time.

We still had our problem with the USSR and just about 90 miles from Florida on the island nation of Cuba a revolution was in progress against the dictator Batista.

A school teacher, who many in our country thought was fighting for freedom, ended up overthrowing Batista on January 1, 1959 and shortly thereafter declared himself a communist. His name was Fidel Castro.

JUNIOR HIGH SCHOOL YEARS

My dad had divorced my stepmother and it was just he and I. During the summer of 1959 we moved in temporarily with my sister in Hammond, IN. As fall approached I needed to get back in school. I was enrolled at Maywood Jr. High, Hammond, IN. As I remember it, I was only one of maybe a dozen white students. That didn't bother me, but the school's curriculum level was about 1 or 2yrs behind what I had already learned. It was so bad that one day when the teacher was out sick, the school had me teach class.

My dad found another place for us to live and we moved back to Black Oak and the Calumet Township school system. I started attending Calumet Jr. High. I had to play a little catch-up since the curriculum was ahead of what was being taught at my previous school. Calumet had a diverse school population. We had students of all races and economic levels and everyone pretty much got along.

In junior high I fell in love with history. It was mandatory that we study state, world, and US history. It soon became rather clear to me that what we are today was because of what had gone on before. We learned about different forms of government, kings, dictators, and the earlier attempts at democracy in Greece and Rome. We also studied how religious beliefs played into the success and failures of various countries. It became clear to me that if you didn't learn from history it had a tendency to repeat itself and it wasn't normally the good stuff that got repeated.

As my junior high school years came to an end, so did Eisenhower's presidency. I think he did a pretty good job. He had built a great highway system, balanced the country's budget three times, ended the hot war in Korea, kept us from going to war with the USSR, and made some advancement on civil rights.

What many of us didn't know was that during his administration other things primarily with the CIA were happening that would play a future role in our lives:

1953 – They over threw the democratic elected government of Iran and installed the Shah.

1954 – In Vietnam, the Saigon Military Mission was overseeing covert psychological and para-military actions.

1954 – Intervention in Guatemala

1958 – Intervention in Indonesia and Lebanon

1960 – Planned invasion of Cuba to overthrow the Castro regime

END OF AN ERA

January 17, 1961, Eisenhower gave his farewell address to the nation. He was a popular president with an approval rating over 60%. If not for the 22nd Amendment to the Constitution (term limit on presidents) he probably could have run for another term and been elected. He warned our country of some important things. From the press release I obtained from the Eisenhower Library I would like to share two pieces of his advice. Most remembered is this:

"In the councils of government, we must guard against the acquisition of unwarranted influence, whether sought or unsought, by the military-industrial complex. The potential for the disastrous rise of misplaced power exists and will persist.

We must never let the weight of the combination endanger our liberties or democratic processes. We should take nothing for granted. Only an alert and knowledgeable citizenry can compel the proper meshing of the huge industrial and military machinery of defense with our peaceful methods and goals, so that security and liberty may prosper together."

Later in his speech he said this:

"Another factor in maintaining balance involves the element of time. As we peer into society's future, we – you and I, and our government – must **avoid the impulse to live only for today, plundering, for our own ease and convenience, the precious resources of tomorrow. We cannot mortgage the material assets of our grandchildren without risking the loss also of their political and spiritual heritage. We want democracy to survive for all generations to come, not to become the insolvent phantom of tomorrow.**"

He also said, ". . . that this world of ours, ever growing smaller, **must avoid becoming a community of dreadful fear and hate, and be, instead, a proud confederation of mutual trust**

and respect." He wasn't just talking about the world but we as Americans in our own country.

My opinion: I think Eisenhower was one of the finest presidents we ever had. He wasn't really a politician (he left the politics of the GOP to his vice-president, Richard Nixon). Under his leadership a lot of good things happened and that was with the opposing party controlling both houses of congress for most of his presidency. Having been a 5-star general officer leading the world in defeating the Nazis in Europe, he had an excellent understanding of the military-industrial complex and the potential dangers associated with it. He was a real American Hero.

CHAPTER 4

John F. Kennedy, Democrat, January 1961 - November 22, 1963

May of 1960 I graduated from Calumet Junior High School. We had a formal graduation ceremony and I remember my dad and new stepmother attending. Dad was really proud of me. I had formally accomplished an educational goal that he never had a chance to do. I spent that summer working my first job other than cutting lawns for 50 cents. I was hired by a guy to sell ice cream from a three wheel bicycle that had a refrigeration unit loaded with ice cream and dry ice. I peddled that bike from early morning until dark selling popsicles, ice cream bars, and ice cream sandwiches, for ten cents each. It was a lot of weight to push around on the bike and I normally covered 10 to 15 miles a day. Talk about taking the weight off of a kid that did. I met a lot of people, kids and adults and never had any problem with anyone. No one ever tried to cheat me or take my money. I learned the value of hard work that summer and did pretty well saving money to buy clothes for the new school year.

A NEW WORLD?

1960 was an election year quite different from previous elections. Senator John F. Kennedy was the Democrat candidate and Vice-President Richard Nixon was the Republican candidate. What made this election really different was it was the first time in our history for televised Presidential Debates. In the first debate, I thought Kennedy came across more confident and smarter that Nixon. Kennedy understood the power of television and prepared for it. Nixon looked like a total wreck, sweating, and arrogant. Unfortunately for him, he had just recently been released from the hospital after injuring his leg which became infected, he didn't rest up and prepare for the debate, and he wouldn't allow makeup for television. We have had televised presidential debates ever since.

Kennedy had something else going for him. He was considered a war hero. During WWII he was skipper of PT109 which was sunk by a Japanese destroyer when the destroyer cut his boat in half and sunk it. Kennedy saved the lives of several crew members including pulling one of the injured who couldn't swim by putting a strap in his own mouth and towing the individual through the water to an island.

While there Kennedy would swim out every night searching for a rescue boat. He eventually came across a native boat and carving a message into a coconut had the native take the message to the Navy resulting in the rescue of his crew. A movie, PT 109 was made that told his story. Not bad when running for office. We all like heroes.

Kennedy did face some obstacles in his election. He was a Roman Catholic and that didn't set too well with many of the Southern Baptist and Lutherans. They felt he would be too obligated to the Pope and many of them didn't even think being Catholic was being a member of the Christian faith (**religious discrimination?**). He was able to overcome it though.

His other obstacle was his age. He was only 43. Only one President had ever been younger when elected and that was Teddy Roosevelt at the age of 42. I thought it was great that someone young was running.

Another problem was he was from the North. Smartly he asked Senator Lyndon Johnson, the powerful Senate Majority Leader from Texas to be his running mate which helped him win the South.

This turned out to be the closest election of the 20th century. Both candidates were popular and drew big crowds. Kennedy won the national popular vote by a little over 112,000 votes, but he won the Electoral College 303 to 219. How did this happen? Kennedy concentrated on the swing states with the electoral votes while Nixon campaigned in all 50 states. Needless to say the Republican Party claimed voter fraud and challenged the results. (**Sound familiar?**).

The primary concern was the vote count in Illinois and Texas. At the time of this election electronic voting machines were not in use. There were some major disputes over the number of people who voted versus the number of people registered to vote in both of these states and the number of people who voted but were dead.

I don't know about Texas at that time, but in Chicago there had always been some questionable shenanigans in elections. The Mafia was big time messing in elections and Chicago Mayor Daley ran the city and the Democrat Party. It was said at that time, that he won the election for Kennedy.

The Democrats still controlled both houses of congress.

Three days after the election Nixon conceded but the RNC continued to challenge the election until mid-1961. Nixon opposed doing this as he felt it could lead to a Constitutional Crisis. He put the country first and I appreciate that kind of thinking and action.

I found Kennedy to be an inspiring speaker. At his January 1961 inauguration he motivated me with his "Ask not what your country can do for you, ask what can you do for your country." I think he really believed what he said. The next day he doubled the quantity of surplus food to needy American families and on March 1st he established the Peace Corps. Considering all the sabre rattling going on in the world, this sounded to me like someone trying to make a positive difference.

CHALLENGING AND TURBULENT TIMES

As I was finishing up junior high, Kennedy faced his first crisis. April of 1961 he went along with a CIA plan originated during the Eisenhower administration to overtly invade Cuba with the help of 1500 Cuban exiles. This was the Bay of Pigs invasion which failed dramatically. It only took 3 days and all 1500 had been killed or captured by Castro's forces.

Kennedy blamed the CIA and the CIA blamed Kennedy for not providing air support to the invaders. Not a very good start to a presidency.

May 25th of 1961 Kennedy really got my attention when he addressed congress with the idea of landing a man on the moon and returning him safely before the decade was out. Now that was something to get a young person excited especially since on May 5th Alan Shepard had just become the first American in space.

As for me, my freshman year at Calumet High School was rather challenging. The school in September 1961 was more oriented towards developing industrial skills than to college prep.

I had already discovered in junior high that my drafting skills and woodworking would not be a future for me. There were classes in automotive maintenance taught at Calumet, but that wasn't an interest of mine either.

English, Algebra, Biology, Latin, and the mandatory Physical Education classes made up my first year. English and PE were my only strong points getting a B grade overall. Otherwise just a

C average student, not quite the Junior Honor Society student that I had been in junior high. I think my first year was just a little intimidating.

My sophomore year was a lot better and I enrolled in my first year of journalism. I thought maybe the world was going to be a lot better. John Glenn became the first American to orbit the earth and Kennedy announced that we were going to go to the moon, but October 14th a U-2 spy plane flying over Cuba detected Soviet missile sites on the island.

Kennedy imposed a naval blockade of the island over ruling the military who wanted to conduct an aerial attack on the sites and we stood at the brink of nuclear war. For the next two weeks we expected to be hit by nuclear bombs. No more duck and cover. No more fallout shelter hopes. Soviet ships were approaching the blockade line. We knew that this would probably be the end of everything. Nothing would save us. Then the miracle happened. The ships stopped and turned away.

Kennedy and Khrushchev reached an agreement. We wouldn't invade Cuba and we would pull our missiles out of Turkey and the Soviets would dismantle the Cuban missile sites and leave Cuba.

We all breathed a sigh of relief and Kennedy's popularity soared. We were all alive and Kennedy had backed the Soviets down. Despite the fact that we still had civil rights issues, mafia killings in our cities, and above ground testing of nuclear weapons, we were in the age of Camelot.

As we entered 1963 the crisis with the Soviet Union may have been resolved but Vietnam was in real turmoil. We sent 16,000 troops to the area and by July it was a full blown crisis. We overthrew the government of President Diem, backing his assassination on November 2.

August of 1963 Kennedy signed the Nuclear Test Ban Treaty with the Soviet Union. No longer would either side be exploding nuclear weapons in the air or in the water. Maybe the world was getting smarter. Maybe I would make it to adulthood. He even was talking to Khrushchev about joint space exploration missions. During the month the "March on Washington" occurred. This was one of the most notable events of the civil rights movement. It was here that Rev. Martin Luther King Jr., gave his famous "I have a dream" speech. I was impressed. There was no violence, just peaceful protests of people asking for what they were entitled to by being US citizens.

November 22nd I was sitting in typing class when the school turned on a radio announcement. President Kennedy was in Dallas and had been shot. We thought he had just been wounded. I remember one of the students saying, "The shooter should have used a shotgun and gotten the job done". What? By the end of the school day we knew the truth. Our president had been assassinated. How could this happen? Why?

When I got home that day from school, my folks had the television on. Walter Cronkite was doing the news when the bulletin came on that the president had died. Everyone was very quiet and it pretty much stayed that way until after his burial. Usually the family would get together for a big Thanksgiving dinner but not that year. There was nothing to celebrate.

When his assassin Oswald was captured and then shot on television while being moved from the Dallas jail, I along with most Americans saw that live on TV. Has the world gone crazy?

Thank goodness we didn't have the internet and social media at the time because rumors and conspiracy theories were running rampart without it. Who was behind it? The Soviets, the Cubans, the CIA, the Mafia, even President Johnson was accused. No one accepted that a lone gunman had done it. The conspiracy theories still go on today.

Lesson learned: What I learned was to not take anything for granted. Even when it seems that the world is on the right track, shit happens! There are a lot of bad people in the world including here, but there are a lot of good people also and just because someone looks different, speaks different, or has different religious believes doesn't mean they are really different.

CHAPTER 5

Lyndon B. Johnson, Democrat, November 22, 1963 – January 1969

On November 22, 1963 following the death of President Kennedy, Lyndon Johnson was sworn in aboard Air Force One as President of the United States. Mrs. Kennedy was standing there next to him as he took the oath of office. I and the rest of the country was stunned by what had occurred but the American government went on as it is supposed to.

I wasn't too sure about LBJ when he became president. I knew he had been tough in the Senate and that he came from Texas. I also knew that he really wasn't liked by the Kennedy family and expected to see whatever President Kennedy had planned wouldn't happen. As it was he did follow through on many things JFK had been striving for, but for some reason I didn't really trust him. He was questioned one time about Vietnam and our involvement there. I remember his statement that, "I will not send American boys to fight a war that should be fought by Asian boys". I looked at my dad and said, "I think I just got screwed".

July 1964 President Johnson signed the Civil Rights Act prohibiting discrimination in employment and education and outlawed racial discrimination in public places. I was impressed that a Democrat from Texas got that done.

The next month the world began to change again. August 5, 1964 in the Gulf of Tonkin it was reported that North Vietnamese torpedo boats had attacked the USS Maddox and USS Turner Joy. The Captain of the Maddox didn't buy it (it was later proved he was right), but the nation did. Vietnam was no longer a backwater in Southeast Asia and would come to dominate our lives for many years.

The following year in March 1965, 3500 Marines landed in Vietnam. I knew that we were going into a real war. Also that month in Selma, Alabama 600 peaceful demonstrators were beaten and tear gassed by the state police that had been sent by Governor George Wallace to break up the demonstration. This was all televised in American homes. It was one of the most vicious attacks I had ever seen in my young life.

President Johnson also pushed what he called "The Great Society". This was going to make our urban areas look good again, improve education, conservation, and included some of the most important laws in American history. Medicare and Medicaid was past. The Voting Rights Act of 1965 ensuring the right of African Americans to vote was past. When he signed it he supposedly said, "We just lost the South". He was right. Before his term in office expired he had lost control of the Democrat Party, the war in Vietnam had worsen and demonstrations against the war were occurring all over the country, and racial tensions was tearing the country apart. This would lead to Strom Thurman and many of the other Dixiecrats eventually joining the Republican Party.

FINAL SCHOOL DAYS

During my junior year of high school a new program was started. It was called Distributive Education. Basically, it was to teach you marketable skills in sales/business. I signed up for the program because I needed to earn some money for clothes, entertainment, and save for buying a car. The teacher was Mr. Tom Dakich who had previously taught me in Junior High School. Since part of the program was finding part-time work for the students enrolled I figured he would take good care of me. He did. He hired me to work at a Taste Freeze that he and his brother owned. Not exactly what I was looking for but I made decent money and ice cream was my favorite food. The second year though, I found a job with Montgomery Ward selling clothing in the men's department.

I was still concentrating in school with my journalism classes and college prep courses hoping someday to be a successful newspaper writer. I was appointed Sports Editor and photographer for the school paper and yearbook. Unfortunately I wrote an editorial one day critical of one of the coaches. I found myself in front of the coach and school principal. I was relieved of my position as Sports Editor and told I could take pictures but no more writing. So much for freedom of the press. I still made the Quill and Scroll National Honor Society for high school journalist and planned on attending Indiana University majoring in Journalism after high school.

RELIGIOUS BELIEVES

It was during my high school years that I made a decision regarding my religious faith. I joined the Methodist church and was very active in it. There was a point in time when I thought I might even become a minister. The youth pastor took an interest in my faith and encouraged me to preach occasionally at the Sunday services. I also was selected by the Gary Post Tribune to be one of three journalism students to write an article in answer to the question of "Should public schools sponsor programs and assemblies in observance of religious events?" Of course all three of us came up with the same answer, yes! I believed that almost all Americans believed in God and that our country was founded by Christian men and women.

UNCLE SAME WANTS YOU!

Back in my high school years it was a common practice for military recruiters to come into the school and give the Armed Services Vocational Aptitude Battery Test (ASVAB). It was sold on the idea that it helped us students identify our potential for successful employment in many areas. Actually it was a recruiting tool for the military. We all took the test and recruiters along with the school counselors would point out our special skills.

Now at the time we still had the military draft. When a guy finished high school and if he was physically qualified, unless he went on to college, or got married and had kids, or was in the military reserve or National Guard, he would get drafted for 2 years in the army. The idea of serving my country in a branch of the military didn't bother me. I felt an obligation to do so. Of course I wanted to have some say so about it, so January 19, 1965 while still in school I enlisted in the Naval Reserve. At the time, unless you were going to school, you did one year with the reserve unit and then went on active duty for two years and returned to the reserve until you completed your six year obligation. I enlisted with the intention of being a Navy Journalist and participated in the Reserve Officer Candidate Program since I was going to go to Indiana University. Unlike the ROTC programs, there was no financial assistance other than your reserve pay equivalent to 4 days of active duty pay.

I applied to Indiana University with a major in Journalism as my goal and was accepted to the Journalism Honors Program. The only problem was that I would have to go to the main campus in Bloomington, Indiana. I graduated from Calumet High School, May 1965 and elected to attend the Northwest Campus in Gary, Indiana which would be cheaper for me and I had to find a job during the summer that would pay enough for me to continue my education.

TIME TO GROW UP

The summer of 1965 before I could do anything else I had a few requirements to meet with the Navy. I went to Navy basic training at Great Lakes, IL. While there I learned what being a low-life-nothing meant. It was hard and meant to be so. They broke you down and then built you back up to be a sailor. During the first two days there, we had two members of our company commit suicide. They hung themselves.

My dad who had served in the Navy and went through boot camp at Great Lakes gave me some advice before I left to go there, "Keep your eyes and ears open, your mouth shut, and move fast when the man tells you to do something and don't volunteer for anything". Best advice I ever got. When they first formed our company up they were asking for volunteers for the various "boot" leadership positions. We had several hotshots that step forward. Boy did they let it go to their head that they were somebody special. At least two of them accidentally ran into a door when they tried to push some people around. Our drill instructor decided they weren't right for the job and asked the company who we wanted to lead us. We picked a black recruit and he did a fantastic job. We started looking pretty good when marching and learning our skills. After that everyone pulled together as a team.

One day I did neglect my dad's advice about volunteering. Our DI asked if anyone knew how to type. I raised my hand and he said fallout Carter you are going to the Brig (that's jail in Navy talk) run by the Marines. I reported to the Brig as ordered and reported to the Marine NCO in Charge. Expecting the worse I was shocked when I wasn't called a shit-bird and instead was asked if I would like a cup of coffee! I had a great day with the Marines. They appreciated someone who could type enough that they offered to fix it so I could stay there for the rest of boot camp. I turned it down. Then just before graduation from boot camp we found out that two members of our company had gone AWOL. Why they couldn't wait just a day or two is beyond me but when the company graduated they got to visit my Marine Corps friends at the brig.

Most of my company after graduation returned to their reserve units but I had elected to do a back to back training assignment and went to Main Side of Great Lakes and reported aboard the USS Amherst. It was a Patrol Craft Escort Radar (PCER) used to provide actual shipboard experience to Naval Reservist on Lake Michigan. We steamed on Lake Michigan practicing gunnery and basic seamanship. Having grown up on Lake Michigan I thought I knew what the lake was like. Nope. Once out in the middle of it, it's just like the ocean and rough a good part of the time. We were a small crew and it was crowded. My bunk was the top one in a stack of maybe 5 and there was a pipe that went right across my stomach when I was lying down. I couldn't even turn over! No one said it would be easy. The fun finally ended and it was time to return home, get back to work and get ready for starting college.

COLLEGE AND WORKING

There's nothing unusual about people working while trying to go to college, especially during the time I am covering although it seemed to me that there were more people going to school that either had family helping them or they had some assistance.

I applied for a job at Inland Steel. Unlike some of the people that were wanting an apprenticeship I just needed a job to earn money for school. I took a job working as a laborer. When I reported to my work section I wasn't exactly welcomed with open arms. I was maybe one of three white guys. Everyone else was a person of color, Black, Mexican, Puerto Rican, and not very educated. They immediately assumed that I came from a family much better off than they were and probably spoiled and afraid of hard work. They soon found out that I came from a family that worked labor all their life just like they were doing. It took a while but I finally proved myself to them and was accepted as one of the guys. Soon it seemed like everyone had to bring something from home that their wife or mom had cooked for me to try. I was too young to go after work for a drink with them, but I did visit a couple of their homes. I was rather shocked at the quality of some of the homes. I thought my family was just making it, but what I saw made me grateful for what I had. It wasn't that they didn't want something better, more out of life for their labor, but it wasn't available to them because of who they were. That's something else that hasn't changed much.

With summer over I went back to work for Montgomery Ward while going to college my first semester. It was pretty tough going with the courses I was taking. I passed but not doing as well as I hoped. When second semester came around I decided to let it go and do my time in the Navy come spring.

ACTIVE DUTY 1966 TO 1968

May of 1966 I reported for active service. I was assigned to the USS Fremont, APA-44 an attack transport ship. She was an old ship from World War II and our job was landing the Marines where ever needed. We were also the flagship for the amphibious command.

Reporting aboard and to the Executive Officer, he asked me what my job was going to be in the Navy. I told him I was trained as a Journalist and had already completed the correspondence course as well as had four years' experience in high school. He laughed and said they didn't have journalist on the Fremont and that I would be assigned to boat group division.

The Fremont had a crew of maybe 300 men (not counting the Marines when they were on board). They were of all races, religions, educational levels, from different parts of the country and walks of life. You are at sea so when you aren't working there is no place to go to get away from anyone. You sleep in an area of maybe 30 to 40 of these people with no privacy. The showers and toilets are all in the same open area. You eat at the same table together when it's time to eat. There is no television, computers, fitness center, or any other recreational facility. Maybe once a week they would breakout the 16mm projector and show a movie in the dining area. You would think this would be a boiling pot for trouble, but it wasn't I would say at least 99.9% of the time. All the while back in the States there were protests, riots, beatings, and murders going on.

What was the difference? We had to get along. We talked to each other about home, family, how we grew up and what we wanted to do in life. We played cards together, shared cigarettes and any snacks we might have. If someone had a guitar we might sit around singing songs or just listening to the people that did. We learned that we had more in common with each other than just the Navy. Think about it. When was the last time you actually talked to someone rather than texting?

The boat group division was the main "fighting arm" of the ship. We had guns on her, one 5-incher, and three quad 40mm anti-aircraft guns but the landing craft was what was important. The division was a top-notch outfit and the Fremont had won the Navy's Amphibious Award 12 years in a row and planned to keep on doing it.

All of us new guys went through an initiation process. You always got the worse bunks (mine was the highest mounted way above a table) when you first got there and they had what was called the order of the pink belly. That meant they would pull the new person out of their bunk and beat on their stomach until they either turned pink or cried. I was watching all this from my bunk, high above the action. I noticed that the guys being initiated wouldn't fight back but just gave in. When my turn came they told me to get down and take my medicine. I told them no, then jumped off my bunk landing on top of the guys and started to fight. That didn't last long but once they had me pinned, it was a love tap not the beating the others had gotten. That's what they were looking for, just to see who would be willing to fight. They wanted to know who they could depend on when needed. After that, we were all brothers. A team pulling together.

It was only a couple of months later that while swabbing the deck that I saw someone on the signal bridge. Having learned semaphore from a friend of mine back at the reserve center, I gave the sign that I wanted to talk and the signalman answered. Soon he came down where I was and asked if I would rather be a signalman and I said yes. The next day I was transferred from the boat group division to the signal bridge. Smart move but whenever we had a landing to make I was always the signalman being sent out with the boats!

My time on the Fremont was exciting. I made several overseas deployments to many countries including Cuba and Jamaica.

We had run-ins with the Soviet Navy many times. It may have been a cold war but they were the enemy. The Russian Navy was a lot newer than any of the ships in our squadron of assault ships and they were aggressive. They would steam into our formations and try to disrupt our formations. Their ships were heavily armed and there was no doubt they could easily sink us if the shooting ever started. Amazingly they knew the names of our

Commodores and ship's Captains. I know this because often when they would pull into our formations I would be taking the message from their commander through their signalmen to our leaders.

Unlike today we didn't have the high tech communication systems. So things like news of what was going on in Vietnam or home wasn't readily available. I knew things were going bad in both places. Many of our Marines were Vietnam Vets and we were training the landing teams that would probably be heading that way after our cruise.

There were two big incidents while in our area of operations. The first was when the six day war broke out and the Israelis shot up one of our spy ships the USS Liberty. I saw the ship and wondered just whose side were the Israelis on. The other incident was when the North Koreans captured the USS Pueblo. The word was we had the only combat landing team afloat and might be ordered to go through the Suez Canal and to Korea to take her back. It didn't happen.

Even though I didn't serve in Vietnam I still got the same treatment as those that did when stateside. Name calling and being spit on happened to all of us at some time or another. I couldn't understand the actual hatred that was shown to those of us serving. It wasn't like we as individuals elected to start a war. The hard feelings generated against many of the protestors are still with members of my generation.

January 30, 1968 the US got caught with our pants down in Vietnam. The North Vietnamese launched the Tet Offensive. It cost the North 60% casualties. Before the year was over we had over 485,000 US troops in Vietnam. By then we had over 20,000 US troops killed in action.

February 27, 1968 Walter Cronkite reported from the war zone that Vietnam would end in a stalemate, which led President Johnson to say, "If I have lost Cronkite, I have lost middle America". He had, and the country was really turning against the war.

March 16, 1968, news of the My Lai massacre was reported. It was a cover-up and only heighten the anti-war movement.

April 4, 1968 we suffered another tragedy. Martin Luther King Jr. was assassinated in Memphis, TN. The news was shattering. A man who preached peaceful protest gunned down by some radical white guy just because of his race and the fact he was working to secure the lawful rights of minority Americans. The hate in this country was just amplified. Racial tensions aboard ship were high and I was surprised that we didn't have a riot aboard ship. There were more riots in the civilian world. America was burning.

In May I took terminal leave from the Navy and went home rather discouraged by what was going on. President Johnson declared he wasn't going to run for re-election and would concentrate on ending the war in Vietnam. Senator Robert Kennedy, brother of slain President Kennedy was running for the Democrat nomination for president. While campaigning in California on June 6th he was assassinated. How much longer was the craziness going to go on? Five days later I was discharged from active duty June 1968.

Lesson learned: It is possible for people to get along together especially when sharing the hazards we face in the world. There is no reason not to bring that experience home and continue it. Despite the positive experience of working with others different than myself in the Navy, I found that when I got home the racial hatred and political hatred was even worse than before.

CHAPTER 6

Richard Nixon, GOP, January 1969 – August 9, 1974

After completing my active duty obligation to the Navy, I returned home feeling like a grown man but somewhat troubled by what I came back to. The country seemed to be falling apart over the Vietnam War and civil rights. The use of drugs and the "free love" movement seemed to have taken over the youth of America. I started back part-time in college and found that veterans were really looked down upon on campus. Even veteran organizations seemed to look at Vietnam era vets differently. I found that many of my friends from high school who served, were experiencing the same thing.

I decided to press on with life and sought my job back with Montgomery Wards. I found out the position I had at the store in Gary, IN was not available, but got lucky and was hired at the store in Munster, IN. I took a position as a commission salesperson in the appliance dept. I was really making some money and it appeared that things were looking up for me. Using my GI Bill, I bought my first house. Several months later I was "promoted" to a department manager position. Nice title, but it turned out to be a pay cut compared to what I made working commission sales. Even so, life seemed good for me but not so much for the country. I eventually left Wards and went to work for Prudential Insurance Company.

WHO IS GOING TO BE PRESIDENT?

With President Johnson deciding not to run for re-election the Democrats were thrown into a quandary. Who would run? Bobby Kennedy was dead and the anti-war movement was strong. It appeared that the anti-war Democrat Eugene McCarthy would be the man, but it was Vice-President Hubert Humphrey who accepted the nomination in Chicago. What a mess that turned out to be. There was somewhere around 10,000 anti-war protesters outside of the convention and they were met by Chicago PD and it was a busting of heads live on TV! The conservative country was really getting fed up with what was going on with all the demonstrations and violence. We needed someone to ride in on the white horse and save America.

"THE SILENT MAJORITY"

Former Vice-President Nixon after losing his first attempt at the presidency to Kennedy, couldn't decide if he wanted to reenter politics or not. It took friends like Reverend Billy Graham to convince him to run. He portrayed himself as someone that represented stability and talked about the "silent majority" of American conservatives who really represented what America was about.

Who was this "silent majority" and what motivated them? I figured that if you voted, you were voicing your opinion, and that wasn't being silent. I think he meant that conservatives weren't speaking loudly enough about their concerns and prejudices. According to the Pew Research Center in the '60s, America was about 85% White, 11% Black, 3.5% Hispanic, and only 0.6% Asian. In 1968 only 60% of eligible citizens that could vote, voted. That was more than the previous Presidential election and it was downhill even more since then until the 2000 election.

MOTIVATING THE SILENT MAJORITY

There were some things to wake up the silent majority such as the "Long Hot Summer" of 1967.

The country experienced approximately 160 riots with over 85 people killed. This was followed in 1968 with 25 riots of which 15 occurred in a 10 day period following the assassination of Dr. Martin Luther King. American cities were burning and people were dying. The rioting and protesting wasn't just about the Vietnam War (which seemed to me be largely white students) but the injustice occurring against minorities who were being deprived of their constitutional rights, deprived of adequate housing, jobs, and opportunity because of the color of their skin. Dr. King tried to wake America up to what was happening and make peaceful changes but not enough people were listening or wanted to accept what he was saying. Consequently, other organizations turned to violence and attempts to overthrow the government. The extreme left had some pretty nasty groups, i.e. the Black Panthers, the Black Liberation Army, and the Weathermen.

The Black Panthers was formed as an armed self-defense group who wanted to protect their people against the KKK and perceived brutality of the police and had stated goals of improving conditions for their people. They also had some extreme communistic and revolutionary ideas.

The group had some internal disagreements over being reformist or revolutionary and their membership declined with many joining the Black Liberation Army.

The Black Liberation Army (BLA) was a truly underground revolutionary group. They claimed to be anti-capitalist, anti-imperialist, anti-racist, and anti-sexist, and strived for a Socialist life for Black people who would have control of their own destiny as a people. Between 1970 and 1976 it is believed they were involved in over 70 violent incidents according to a Justice Department report on BLA activities. It is also believed they were responsible for the assassination of at least 13 police officers.

The Weathermen or Weather Underground was a faction of the Students for a Democratic Society (SDS). The SDS itself was rather Democratic Socialist in their thinking and they primarily participated in peaceful protest against the war in Vietnam and were supportive of the civil rights movement and wanted to improve life for the poor to include economic and security benefits. It started on the campus of the University of Michigan. The Weathermen however desired to form a revolutionary party to overthrow the government for what they called American Imperialism. This was a bad group, probably the worst or close to the worse at the time. Besides their support of black power and opposition to the war, they wanted a new government. They even issued a "Declaration of War" against the US Government. They allied themselves with the Black Liberation Movement and other radical groups to see to "the destruction of "US Imperialism" and the institution of a classless communist world".

They didn't fool around. They were responsible for the bombing of government buildings, corporate buildings, and banks. They attacked the US Capitol building, the Pentagon, and the US Department of State building. Believe it or not they even exploded a bomb at the headquarters of the New York City Police! They had planned a bombing attack against soldiers and NCOs having a dance at Ft Dix. They met with North Vietnamese representatives in Cuba and accepted money, training and tactics, and explosives from Communist Cuba. They didn't quite achieve the street recruiting goals that they hope for but they did have three collectives of one each in California, New York City, and the Midwest. They concentrated on recruiting high school and college students believing they could easily bring these people around to their way of thinking.

The Weathermen pretty much fell apart by 1977 but some members went on and robbed banks and Brink trucks until captured.

NIXON WINS

Nixon was pretty smart. He knew he needed Southern and Western conservatives to win. He selected Spiro Agnew, the governor of Maryland to be his running mate to appease the South and promised to appoint conservative judges. He and Agnew ran a terrific media campaign with commercials and personal appearances. He blamed the high crime rate on the Democrats and promised "peace with honor" in Vietnam, and restore strength over the Soviet Union by regaining nuclear superiority. He said he would restore law and order, crackdown on illegal drugs, and end the draft. Conservatism would return to America. It was a three way race between Nixon, Humphrey, and George Wallace a former Democrat and racist segregationist, who ran as an independent. I was a fiscal Conservative Republican and although a little leery of Nixon voted for him. He was sworn in as President

January 20, 1969. The GOP had won the presidency, but the Democrats controlled both houses of congress for the entirety of his presidency.

NEW FEDERALISM

Nixon had to find a way to appease his supporters in the south and came up with what was called New Federalism. He established state controlled desegregation of schools by establishing biracial committees to plan and implement their own policies. It made a significant difference.

Nixon also increased the number of female appointees in his administration and had sex discrimination guidelines added to federal contracts.

In 1970 he pushed for the Clean Air Act, and established the Department of Natural Resources and the Environmental Protection Agency. He also created the Office of Safety and Health Administration (OSHA).

He tried to restrict federal spending and provided state and local governments with billions of federal tax dollars. Although successful at first, he ended up with huge deficits in his budgets, high inflation, increasing unemployment, and trade deficits.

FIRST TERM SUCCESS/FAILURES

July 20, 1969 we beat the rest of the world in reaching the moon. Neil Armstrong and Buzz Aldrin walked on the moon. It was the most exciting thing to happen in the world, up to that point. Despite all that was going on in the country and the world I think we all pulled together as one that day. President Nixon showed a sense of humor when he called the astronauts during their mission to congratulate them. I remember laughing when he concluded the call saying he needed to hang up as he was calling long distance.

Nixon spoke to the public and told us how we would keep all our commitments to our allies. He said he would return greater authority to the state and local governments and did.

He told us in November 1969 that he had a plan to honorably end the war in Vietnam. Unfortunately that didn't happen and instead we expanded the war into Cambodia April 1970 and the anti-war demonstrations went nationwide over it. May 5, 1970 the students at Kent State University in Ohio had a peaceful protest but the National Guard was called in. I don't think anyone knows for sure what caused it but the National Guard opened fire killing four students and wounding nine others. My thought was what the hell is going on in America?

President Nixon was definitely anti-communist and knew you couldn't trust the USSR. He took advantage of the fact that China and the USSR were having some strong disagreements. In an effort to shift the cold war balance of power to the west he entered into secret communications with the Chinese. Lifting the trade restrictions on China led to the Chinese inviting the US table tennis team for competition. The press called it "ping-pong diplomacy" but it worked. He became the first president to visit China and threw a monkey wrench into the Soviet plans for world domination.

Because of the war we were experiencing domestic inflation. He tried to solve the problem by restricting government spending but his budget ran the deficit into billions of dollars, the largest in our country's history at the time. Not exactly what a fiscal conservative wanted to hear. He cut the defense budget in half, once again not exactly what a conservative wants to hear. After all we still had the Soviet Union to deal with. He also imposed wage and price controls which no one wanted to hear. He did meet with the Soviet Premier and reached an agreement called SALT (Strategic Arms Limitation Talks) which was to dissuade the Soviets from a first strike against us.

I thought at the time that he was doing pretty good job though and was quick to blame the Democrat congress for the failures.

LIVING THE GOOD LIFE

As I mentioned earlier, I got out of the Navy spring of 1968. In the Navy as a 3rd class petty officer, I earned a whopping $120 a month and that included sea-pay. Obviously I was looking for substantially more as a civilian and since continuing college was no longer in the picture, I returned to a civilian occupation that I knew I was really good at, sales.

Now understand I was in my very early twenties and single. At first I worked at Montgomery Wards, but a friend of mine convinced me to consider Prudential as an agent. I had bought my first home for a little over $20,000 with a $220 a month house payment (my dad thought I was crazy taking that on) and a brand new 1968 Olds

Cutlass convertible. The median income in the US at that time was $8600. Taking inflation into consideration, $1 in 1968 is equivalent to $7.60 today. I was making over $10,000 a year. You can do the math. Many of my friends from high school were making a lot less than that and working in the steel mills. My normal apparel was a suit and I bought nice suits. Material things were pretty important and that was how people judged you. It was wine, women, and song as the old saying goes.

My district manager at Prudential was a real gentleman and during my employment interview found out he had been my dad's insurance agent years earlier. He gave me a great opportunity and I took it. Interestingly enough it turned out that the agents were unionized and were threatening to go on strike to get more money for collecting premiums for the company. We were what were called debit agents meaning we visited with the clients monthly to collect their premiums. I wasn't too excited about the idea of going on strike on a brand new job. It turned out that during my 3 month probationary period I couldn't join the union anyway. I was approached by the union representative and was told that if they went on strike, even though I didn't belong to the union, I would also have to walk out and not sell any insurance or collect any premiums. I told him he was crazy and that I would work no matter what. That's when he made the mistake of saying that if I didn't support the strike, that beautiful convertible might have something happen to it. That's when I looked him in the eye, pulled back my coat jacket and showed him that I was wearing a .357 magnum revolver and suggested that he might want to make sure nothing happened to my car or I might be visiting him. No union was going to keep me from earning a living. I never had much use for unions after that. I told my district manager that the union had threaten me and I wouldn't join. He understood how I felt but told me that I would have to join no matter what when my probationary period was over. Fortunately there was no strike.

Prudential was a great company to work for but management had some quirks. For instance you should always wear conservative suits, white shirts, and non-flashy ties. They were also a little concerned that I drove a sporty convertible rather than a more conservative family car and of course the fact I was single was a little unsettling.

I overcame their concerns pretty quick with the amount of new policies I was writing. Next thing you know it was okay that I and the younger agents dressed a little more updated than they did.

Even though I was licensed to sell insurance anywhere in Indiana, I was assigned to Crown Point (the county seat for Lake County) along with another agent that I will just call Paul. We had worked together at Montgomery Wards and were real friends. Paul and I were close in age and he was a former Marine. Because of our military background our staff manager insisted that we join the American Legion Post in town. It didn't take long to get to know a lot of influential people in Crown Point including agents with other companies. The Legion Post became our hangout when we finished working for the day and increased my exposure and involvement in the community.

The majority of the Post membership were World War II vets. As great as the guys were there was some bad vibes when it came to how they felt about the Korean War and Vietnam War veterans. No one certainly didn't care much for the current generation protesting the war. Most often protestors were referred to as "Long hair, hippy, communist, pink-o freaks". At the same time there wasn't much sympathy for the civil rights movement since we had cities burning all over the country. Something in my gut told me that we in America were on a downhill slide and that I might find myself defending my country again, but not overseas.

One evening my friend Paul and I were invited to a meeting at the bank. We didn't know who was holding the meeting but that it would be a political discussion with some leaders in the community. We went. After being greeted by some of the people in attendance, we were handed literature about the group. The literature was filled with cartoons showing black men with big lips shooting police officers and describing how all this civil rights stuff was communist propaganda. It was a meeting of the John Birch Society! I threw their literature down and told them they were crazy and walked out. I never got another invite.

Life continued on successfully. I had one client who was the leading real estate broker in Crown Point. I had actually bought two house from him and we became good friends. We would get together for lunch at his office and play cards and just talk about life. He had been a bomber pilot during WWII and belonged to my Legion Post. One day during our conversation he said that he wished he had never left the service. I was kind of shocked and said, "You kidding? You are very successful and well respected in the community. Why would you wish that?" He proceeded to explain to me that there is more to life than making money and having things. He talked about the comradeship and purpose in life that he felt while serving in the Army Air Force. That was more important than money and things. He said if I was your age I would still be serving. I thought about what he said and agreed that he had a good point.

Sometime later in the year, Paul and I were at the Post when we had a visitor come in wearing a DAV (Disabled American Veterans) hat. As the only Post officer present I went down introduced myself and Paul and offered to pay for his first drink which was customary at our Post for visiting legionnaires. He asked about our backgrounds, what branch we had served in, and if we were still serving in the reserve. We both said no we weren't in the reserve since we had completed our six year obligation. He was an older guy, a WWII vet and said we should consider maybe joining his USAF reserve unit. We both said no, it would be men, women, and children before they would get us again especially in the reserve doing nothing. He didn't give up though and invited us to visit his unit and see what they were all about and then make a decision. He promised that we would find this unit was a little bit different than what we were thinking. We took him up on his offer and showed up at Grissom AFB one weekend. He was the First Sergeant of the 931st Combat Support Squadron, 434 Special Operations Wing. He introduced us to many members of the outfit which included a ton of WWII vets. They told us about their mission, the aircraft they had, and how their deployments were a lot different than most reserve units. We were sold and Paul and I both joined the outfit. Paul had been a small arms instructor in the Marine Corps and that's the career field they put him in. Me, they had somewhat of a problem. I had been a signalman in the Navy, not quite an Air Force job. "Can you type?" I was asked. I was made an administrative specialist (Sgt E-4) and went to work for the First Sergeant that had recruited us.

I really enjoyed being back in the military environment again even if it was only one weekend a month. The comradeship was intoxicating. One weekend in the middle of winter I took my wife with me and introduced her to the unit. We had a terrible snowstorm hit and spent most of the weekend helping each other keep our vehicles operable so we could go home Sunday night. My wife who was a school teacher, watched how we all worked together and how I reacted to being part of the unit. On our way home she spoke to me about how happy I seemed to be compared to what I did for a living. I was shocked when she asked if I ever wished I was back on active duty. I honestly said that I did but there was a big difference in what I would earn versus what I made in sales. She said maybe I should think about it. Nixon had got the military a significant pay increase. Remember I said as an E-4 in the Navy that I made $120 a month? Time had changed things. As an E-4 in the Air Force I would make around $600 a month of which $165 would be a tax free housing allowance, plus free medical, dental, a cost saving commissary (food store), and Base Exchange (full service retail store), plus a club and recreational facilities. After having served a year with the 434 SOW, we decided I should go back in, I enlisted in the Regular Air Force.

Now even though I was already in the Air Force Reserve, I still had to go to Chicago and process through the Armed Forces Entrance and Examination center. I get dressed in my suit (typical me) and drive up. Reporting in I find that I am going through the line with a bunch of draftees (if not the last group, pretty close) because even though ending the draft was a promise of Nixon it didn't happen right away. There was a young army private that was yelling at the people processing, including me. I guess because of how I was dressed and definitely older than the rest he decided to take a special interest in me. He came over to give me a hard time and you should have seen the look on his face when I bristled and asked if he always addressed NCOs as he was me. That got his attention and everyone else. With an apology I was separated from the draftees and moved along on my own. After going through the medical exam I had to meet with the doctor. He looked at me and my age and said "I can get you out of this. You aren't one of these kids and shouldn't be drafted." He was shocked when I told him I wasn't a draftee. I was cleared to come back in.

I was sent to a room and told to wait and that an NCO would be talking to me about where I wanted to be assigned, but they needed to get the draftees processed, sworn in and shipped out. Hurry up and wait is an old military axiom and it was true that day. After several hours of just sitting, I got up and found an NCO and discovered they had forgotten that I was waiting. Sitting down with the NCO handling my assignment, I was asked where I wanted to go and said Vietnam. He told me that it was policy that prior service guys had to be back on active duty at least a year before they could be considered for Vietnam or any overseas assignment. So I picked Strategic Air Command (SAC) because they were the front line against the Soviet Union our main enemy and ended up being assigned back to Grissom AFB, 3rd Airborne Command Control Squadron (3rd ACCS). Going to another room I was to wait with several others to be sworn in. As I was sitting there I noticed a guy on the other side of the room that looked awfully familiar. I walked over and said excuse me but were you ever on the USS Fremont as a Marine Sergeant? Sure enough it was someone that I had had a run in with back in those days. We talked about it and I assumed he was going back into the Corps but he too was enlisting USAF. Small world.

Reporting in to 3rd ACCS I was interviewed by the First Sergeant and Commander. The First Shirt wanted to know if I had a problem working for a Black NCO. I was really surprised to be asked that, and said no. Apparently things had changed since my Navy days and even the active military was having serious racial problems. My new boss (NCOIC) was a great guy and I learned a lot about my career field which was important because I didn't really know much about being an admin specialist. The First Sergeant had selected me for the squadron orderly room because he picked up that I was "more military" than most in the unit.

NIXON'S REELECTION

About ten months into my assignment with 3rd ACCS, I get a computer generated punch card saying that I am "Frozen for an overseas assignment". I didn't have any idea what that meant and went to base personnel to find out. I was told that it meant sometime within the next six months I would involuntarily be sent overseas. I asked if it was too late to volunteer so that I would maybe have some say-so about where I would go. Being told yes, I said I wanted Vietnam. I was told no I couldn't go to Vietnam. They gave me an assignment preference sheet (dream sheet is what we called it) and told me to pick out what countries I wanted to go to. It would be an accompanied tour (meaning I could take dependents) and it would be a long tour (meaning four years). I selected anywhere in Europe. Two months later a received orders for Hawaii, PACAF Headquarters, working for the Deputy Chief of Staff for Plans, a 2 star General. Shortly thereafter with the on-going draw down in Vietnam we were changed to DCS Plans and Ops, and then DCS Operations and Intelligence. Every day I was handling messages from units in Vietnam and things didn't match up with what was being reported daily in the news. Even though troops were being withdrawn the USAF and Special Operations were heavily involved.

While all this was going on I and a bunch of us from PACAF Hqtrs, civilian, officers, and enlisted were sent to what was called Race Relations Training. We were all sitting in a half circle in the classroom for discussions. The instructor started going around the room asking why we thought we were there. There was a full Colonel seated next to me and when it was his turn to answer he gave the perfect company answer. I was next. When asked why I thought I was there, my answer was that recently there had been a riot on a base and some buildings were set on fire scaring the hell out of the Air Force and so leadership thought maybe something had better be done. The instructor, a Black Master Sergeant replied, "At last an honest man". The military is and always will be a reflection of the civilian community they come from. It was no different than it is now.

I was fortunate enough to be at Hickam AFB when the war officially ended and our POWs came home. When the plane landed at Hickam AFB there were a few tears shed with the cheers.

Like most Americans I voted for Nixon's re-election. It was a landslide with him carrying approximately 60% of the popular vote and 520 votes in the electoral college (according to Politico). Agnew was to continue as his Vice-President. Agnew wasn't very well liked and was always attacking the press. Publicly he was the nasty face of the administration. It turned out he was also a crook that accepted bribes as VP. He was forced to resign from office in fall of 1973.

This was just the start of the downfall of Richard Nixon.

During the re-election campaign Nixon's organization for some reason was concerned about the democrats who didn't have a chance, and became involved in political sabotage and covert espionage. This lead to the Watergate Break-in. Initially, I didn't think too much about it and there was a radio host in Hawaii who remarked, "Come on folks, don't you think even George Washington probably had a wine glass up against the wall to hear what his opponents were talking about?" We all laughed about it.

It turned out not to be a laughing matter. The press started obtaining inside information about what had happened. The Senate opened hearings. Nixon grew madder and madder about what was happening. His enemies list was growing. He tried everything to stop the investigation and refused to cooperate with the investigation. He claimed to the American public that he knew nothing about the Watergate break-in and that he wasn't a crook. Claiming "Executive Privilege" he refused to release records pertaining to the investigation. The Supreme Court disagreed with his belief that he didn't have to cooperate with Congress and it all came apart for him. The secret White House tape recordings of all conversations in the Oval Office came out and proved he knew and supported all that had gone on with Watergate and his attempts to cover it up. He tried everything to obstruct the investigations but it didn't work including trying to use the CIA to block the FBI investigation. The House Judiciary Committee passed the first of three articles of impeachment. It took the senior Republican leaders in the Senate to convince him to resign from office in-lieu of impeachment which would have found him guilty. He resigned. It came as a shock to many of us that trusted and believed in him. Even when he was caught and had to resign he didn't believe he had done anything wrong. In a later interview he would state that when a President does something it is legal because he is the President. No accountability. My opinion, that's how dictators think, not the President of the United States. I found that pretty scary.

Following the Constitution, Gerald Ford, who was selected by Nixon as his Vice-President with the consent of Congress upon the resignation of Agnew, became President of the United States.

Lesson learned: There is more to life than just money and possessions: Duty, honor, country for a start. Not all politicians have the best interest of the country as being first on their list of priorities. They want personal power and will do anything to get it and keep it. **No one is above the law** even though no legal action was taken because he had resigned and Ford pardoned him. This action would come to haunt us later.

CHAPTER 7

Gerald Ford, GOP, August 9, 1974 – January 1977

Around the time of the Paris Peace Accords were being signed in 1973 which ended offensive operations by the US in Vietnam, I was promoted to Staff Sergeant. We began the withdrawal of forces and started the drawdown of the number of personnel in the military. I felt that President Nixon had kept his promises to the American people. December 6, 1973 Gerald Ford had been made Vice-President filling the vacancy created with Agnew's resignation October1973. I thought maybe the country would get back to normal. However, the truth of what had been going on with Watergate was coming out and Nixon was forced to resign in August 1974. Ford was sworn-in August 9th. He became the only person in American history to fill the office of Vice-President and President without being voted in by the American public. The office of Vice-President would remain vacant through December 19, 1974, when Nelson Rockefeller was made VP.

TRYING TO CLEAN UP THE MESS

If there was ever a politician that I felt sorry for it was Gerald Ford. He didn't seek the office of VP or President but by following the Constitution ended up with the mess created by Nixon. The Democrats still controlled both houses of congress. So, now we have a country seriously divided because of the war and racial divisions and a disgraced former President facing possibly criminal charges. How do you put Humpty-Dumpty back together again so the nation can heal?

In September '74, Ford took two steps that he thought would heal the country. First, he pardoned Richard Nixon for any crimes he might had committed while in office. He thought that would save the country from going through a high visibility and decisive trial that would have prolonged the agony of Watergate. Second, he granted "Conditional Amnesty" for military deserters and draft dodgers. Neither of these actions went over very well with me or other conservatives and the American people in general. As expected there were rumors of a conspiracy between Ford and Nixon that the pardon was granted only so Ford could be President by letting Nixon off the hook.

October wasn't much better as Ford asked for and promoted a 5% tax increase on corporations and wealthy individuals with inflation at a 12% rate. Not exactly what Republicans were known for doing especially with mid-term elections scheduled for the next month.

In November the Republican Party took a licking. They lost 49 more seats in the House, which was already controlled by the Democrats and gave the Democrats a 61 seat majority in the Senate. The Democrats could now easily overcome any Presidential veto.

December was the start of a real downturn in Vietnam. The North Vietnamese decided to test and see how committed we were to the government of South Vietnam and the "Vietnamization of the war program". Even though we had withdrawn our forces from Vietnam in accordance with the Paris Peace Accords, we did supply and provide the assets for the South to defend themselves. On December 13th the North invaded Phuoc Long Providence, only 62 miles from Saigon. I was still assigned to the DCS Operations and Intelligence at PACAF

Headquarters. We could see the writing on the wall. We were doing our best to build up the Vietnamese Air Force to protect themselves. Aircraft were being stripped from units in the States and turned over the Vietnamese. Surely, they could fight off the North.

THE VIETNAM WAR COMES TO AN END

April 23, 1975 President Ford gave a speech at Tulane University. In his speech he stated that "The Vietnam War is over as far as the US is concerned". He was met with applause and cheers. Six days later the North attacked Saigon and the evacuation of Saigon began. It was a disaster in Vietnam. We evacuated over 1000 Americans and thousands of Vietnamese. It was panic in the city as people were trying to get out of country. Helicopters were carrying evacuees to aircraft carriers off shore. It didn't take long before the flight decks were so packed that they had to push choppers overboard so others could land, and in many cases South Vietnamese pilots were crashing the helicopters into the water because there was no space for landing. On the news was the film of the last helicopter evacuating the last Americans from what was reported to be the roof of the US Embassy, actually it was the CIA headquarters.

A month later the Khmer Rouge in Cambodia seized a US merchant ship the Mayaguez. President Ford ordered a rescue mission to secure the captured crew. It was a hodgepodge of US Marines, Air Force Security Police, and Navy. It wasn't known at the time but the crew was being released. We went in and it was a disaster. The rescue mission landed on the wrong island that was heavily armed. We lost 3 helicopters, 18 personnel killed, and over 60 wounded. During the evacuation of rescue mission, 3 Marines got left behind. They were captured and executed. I saw the intelligence reports and films of the operation and was completely devastated. The KIA were added to the Vietnam War Memorial. The war was over. The participants were not eligible for the Vietnam Service Medal.

Note: During the Vietnam War there were always rumors of white people fighting alongside the North Vietnamese troops. None of these "ghosts soldiers" were every reported killed or captured. The same held true of aerial engagements. In the years since it has come out that over 8000 Soviet officers and NCOs did fight against us in Vietnam.

ASSASSINATION ATTEMPTS

September 1975 was a terrible month for President Ford, but proved he was a lucky man. On the 5th, Lynette "Squeaky" Fromme, a follower of the murderer Charles Manson, shot at close range a semi-automatic pistol at President Ford. She missed and before she could fire a second shot a Secret Service agent grasped the gun from her. Seventeen days later another woman, Sara Jane Moore attempted to assassinate the President with her shot just missing his head and this time a former Marine in the crowd was able to grab the gun and keep her from making another shot. The really weird thing is that at one point and time she had been an FBI informant and that just the day before she had been arrested for possession of a firearm but had been released. She had bought the gun used in the assassination attempt, the day she tried to kill the President, but it turned out that the sights were off just a little bit, which saved Ford's life.

ALOHA TO HAWAII

With the drawdown of the US military many of the long tours of 4yrs overseas were reduced to 3yrs. I decided to apply of recruiting duty and got accepted. December of 1975 I transferred from

Hawaii and went on leave prior to going to recruiting school. A new adventure was to begin.

RECRUITING IN WISCONSIN

I had selected Wisconsin for my recruiting assignment, specifically I wanted Greenbay, WI. Where else would a Packer fan want to go? It looked like I had my dream assignment but due to some hiccup on my orders I was delayed and someone else got that slot. I was assigned to Kenosha, WI even though my office was located in Racine, WI.

At the time I reported in the recruiting units were listed as detachments, not squadrons. My new commanding officer was a captain that was a former enlisted marine. I smartly saluted and presented my orders. The captain looked at me and asked, "Sergeant Carter are you extreme left or extreme right?" "I beg your pardon sir?" I replied. "Politically Sergeant". "Well sir, I would say I am more in the middle". "Well Sergeant that won't work in Wisconsin. You are either a Nazi or a Communist". Oh boy, what have I gotten into? Then because I was recently divorced the Operations Superintendent called me aside to let me know that he would personally interview any females that I enlisted to insure I wasn't fooling around with them. I took offense to that even being said and replied, "Well Sarge you don't have to worry about that since female recruits don't count toward my goal, I won't be working any."

After completing my in-processing I was escorted to Racine to meet my new office partner and get situated in my office. My supervisor said he would get back with me in a few days to start my on-the-job training and left. My office partner wasn't around. Soon the phone rang and I answered it. I get someone telling me that he is Congressman Les Aspin and would like some of those big desk calendars that the Air Force gave out, for his staff. Right, let's play a joke on the new guy. I told him I was sorry but with all the cuts to the military we just couldn't give away stuff to everyone and hung up. My phone rings again and there is a female on the phone with a beautiful voiced telling me that she was Congressman Aspin's secretary and he would really appreciate if I could bring three calendars to his local office. Okay, I will fall for it because it might be interesting to meet the person with this great voice. She tells me where the office is at and away I go. Imagine my surprise when I walk-in and the secretary says that the congressman will see me now! Uh oh! He turned out to be a nice guy and I apologized explaining why I had talked to him the way I did.

When I got back my office partner was there. I told him what happened and he just about died laughing. Since all the different branches of military recruiters were located in the same building he took me around and introduced me to everyone and of course told them what I had done. The recruiters were all male and over the years some great friendships were made.

After a few days I got tired of waiting on my supervisor to come down from Milwaukee to start my training and just went to work. Following my partner's guidance I got busy going out visiting the high schools that I was responsible for and introducing myself to the school counselors. I explained Air Force policy that we wanted their students to finish school and I wasn't there to talk anyone into quitting and joining the Air Force. It was a pretty good reception at most of the schools except one.

I had a large Catholic high school in my area. I went there and introduced myself and explained our policy about staying in school and graduate. The principal looked at me and said "come with me". We walked down the hall and he stopped in front of a bunch of pictures. "These were students that were killed in Vietnam and you aren't welcome here." This is a great start.

The next thing I find out is that the USAF is not very popular in the counties I am responsible for. It turned out that in the '50s they were going to build an Air Force base named after the WWII fighter pilot and Medal of Honor winner, Major Richard Bong in Brighton, WI, part of my area. The Air Force took over about 6,000 acres of farm land and homesteads. Roads were torn up and rerouted, and all the big plans for what would have been growth for the area went down the tubes when it was decided that the base wasn't needed after all. On top of this the government kept the land. It wasn't until 1978 that the state of Wisconsin was able to buy the land back for the Bong Recreational Area.

Despite the start of my assignment being a little weird, it was a great place to live and work. My office was right on Lake Michigan. You didn't have to go very far for fantastic fishing and if that wasn't enough there were plenty of rivers for fishing and camping. Friday nights were great because almost all the taverns had fish fries.

Fresh lake perch and all you could eat. I really took advantage of that and quiet often was asked "don't they feed you boys in the Air Force?" "Not like this" I would reply.

Kenosha and Racine counties were real blue-collar worker areas. We had an AMC plant which built cars and jeeps. Two big corporations, Caterpillar and Johnson and Johnson had facilities located there. Most of the rest of the area depended on farming and tourism. Lake Geneva, WI is a good example.

Not everything was nice. We had some biker groups in the area and illegal drugs caused many problems. With the mafia being in Chicago and Milwaukee there would be an occasional killing.

It was 1976 which was the Presidential election year. Ford was talked into running for the Republican nomination. He was opposed by the Governor of California, Ronald Reagan. Personally I supported Reagan, but Ford won the nomination. The Democrats selected a Georgia Peanut farmer and former governor Jimmy Carter.

After several weeks, my flight supervisor (we were called flights for organizational purposes) started working with me and saw that I seemed to take to the position like a fish to water. He told me one thing I needed to do was hold a Center of Influence (COI) event. A dinner somewhere for my school counselors. I think I was authorized like $150 for the dinner and was told we couldn't buy alcohol with Air Force money. Okay. I arranged a dinner at the Lake Geneva Playboy Resort. They took good care of me with a special rate because I was military. I dug into my own pocket and put up another $100 of my own money for an open bar. When we had the dinner my guest were loving it, but my supervisor about had a heart attack when the bar opened. He took me aside about the bar. "I told you the Air Force can't buy drinks!" I told him I was buying the drinks. "Well, you had better make sure that they know that."

When I went up front to address the crowd I mentioned about the Air Force policy and that USAF was not paying for the drinks, but "Uncle Jimmy" hopes you remember him come fall. Laughter and applause.

At that time to enter the Air Force we had a policy that if you had ever smoked marijuana more than 3 times, you were automatically disqualified. I was a little bit tougher. As far as I was concerned if you had ever smoked marijuana I didn't need you in MY Air Force. My supervisor didn't like that either, even though I met and exceeded assigned goals all the time. He reminded me that I didn't set the standard. Eventually the Air Force changed the standard to "have you used marijuana within the last 6 months?" We were also tougher on the physical and mental requirements to qualify for enlistment. Statistically only 1 out of 5 that wanted to enlist would qualify. Anyone that failed for USAF I would normally take them over to one of the other services where the requirements weren't so stringent, but even then the number of high school graduates who couldn't qualify for the military was pretty high. It seemed that reading and math was a big weakness, but drugs and law problems were more than abundant.

IT WAS A PEOPLE BUSINESS, GOOD AND BAD

A lot of people thought being a recruiter would be a knock job. After all, weren't they standing in line to join? No they weren't. Even though the unemployment rate was around 9% finding qualified people for the USAF was a 24/7 mission to me. Unless I was hunting, fishing, or participating in sports I was generally always in uniform meeting and talking with people. It wasn't like today where you do most of the work on a computer, you actually spent facetime with people and got known in the community. Most of the time it was fun for me. I was known for having a sense of humor (sometimes dark) because it was really necessary dealing with all kinds of people.

I can't even guess how many talks I gave during this timeframe to civic groups, radio stations, newspaper interviews, or how many parades and patriotic events I participated in. Because of my earlier background as a Scoutmaster, I was asked to be the District Commissioner. I was invited to visit many of the Scout troops and they always wanted me to come in my Air Force uniform and inspect the scouts. I and my office partner helped out with many of the charity groups doing fund raisers and that was very rewarding and great public relations building trust in the community. Besides these activities I had monthly school visits to make and also participated in what was basically job fairs at schools and with the state employment agency.

I remember all the recruiters being asked to participate in an Alternative High School college and job fair event. We all knew that we would probably be wasting our time but the counselor at the school was also the counselor for one of our largest regular high schools and no one wanted to turn her down. I was doing my normal thing with a table set up and a portable audio visual machine showing recruiting films when I noticed that the Army recruiters had packed up and were leaving. I asked them why and they told me to walk down the hall and see what one teacher had done. I did and when I read a poster the teacher had put up on the wall I just had to go tell the Marine recruiter. "Gunny, I think we have a former marine teaching here. He has a poster up, something about "A Few Good Men" the USMC recruiting slogan. Gunny gets all puffed up and strides down the hall. When he gets there he sees the poster which read "Here's why they are looking for a few good men!" it was the casualty figures for every war we had fought since the revolutionary war. Gunny reached up, pulled the poster down and tore it up. Stomping back he looked at me and said, "Well I guess I showed him!" I waited a little bit and walked down again. Sure enough the teacher had replaced the poster. Smiling I went back and told the Gunny the poster had returned. He stomped down the hall and tore it down again and had a few words with the teacher. He came back, told the Navy about it and they both packed up and left. Now I am the only service left. I walk down the hall and sure enough the poster is up again and the teacher is standing there with his arms folded and a whole bunch of students watching to see what will happen. I stand there studying the poster and said. "Wow, someone really did a lot of research on this. I am not sure but I bet the information is correct." The teacher smiles, and the kids get a little more alert. I go "you know this is really interesting because it appears that in all the major wars the average number of deaths on our side per year seem to go down compared to the wars before them and you know in one year almost as many people are killed on the US highways as we lost in Vietnam during the entire 20 year war. It must be because the US military today, is the best trained, highest motivated, and best supported in the history of our country." The teacher tore his sign down and returned to his classroom slamming the door. I packed up my stuff and left.

I have always had a special respect for the Marine Corps, probably because of my Navy days on an attack transport hitting the beach with them and have always had fun kidding with them. So no disrespect intended to any Marines reading this.

ANOTHER GOTCHA

It was a hot, summer Saturday and I'm walking into the office when I notice some people standing on the street corners near the office and on the sidewalks stopping people and handing out leaflets. I go in and stop by the Marine recruiting office. "Hey Gunny, are those your people outside handing out literature? "What are you talking about?" he asked. I told him to go take a look. He came storming back in and asked if I knew who they were and I said, "Yes, they are Nazis is full uniform, riot style helmets, with batons." Gunny, wanted to go out a kick some butt. I told him to settle down there is nothing we can legally do about it. I guess the Captain was right, when I joined the unit. Definitely had some Nazis believers in the neighborhood.

Sometimes though, there are humorous political based stories. It is the Wisconsin State Fair and of course USAF Recruiting has a booth setup. Jimmy Carter was in his first year as President. I was working the booth along with a female Air Force Reservist. We were relieved to grab something to eat and walk around the fair. We are walking in to where they had a flower show going on when this guy walks up, grabs my hand and says, "Hello Mr. Carter I am Bill Proxmire, your Senator." Smiling I replied, "Well Senator I'm not a mister but Staff Sergeant Carter and you aren't my Senator because I'm from Indiana." He got the point and then says, "Sergeant Carter …, any relation to the President?" I replied, smiling once again, "You mean Uncle Jimmy?" laughing the young lady and I walked on in to the flower show. A few months later Senator Proxmire was in Racine and stopped by my office. He told me he saw my uncle the other day and told him what a great job I was doing for the Air Force. That was probably a gotcha on his part, but who knows. Even though, he was known to give his Golden Fleece Award for government waste to agencies including DOD and the Air Force and was a Democrat, I thought he was a pretty nice guy.

PRESIDENT FORD LOSES THE ELECTION

Like I said at the beginning I felt sorry for Ford, the man. I am sure he was a great congressman for Michigan but he bumbled more that any Presidential candidate that I was ever aware of. Asking in October '74 for a tax increase and then 7 months later proposing a $16 billion tax cut was enough to cause a pause in the voter's mind. Even though he was remembered being athletic in his youth, he actually stumbled a few times getting off of Air Force One and of course it was on camera. Everyone remembered his pardon of Nixon and that didn't go over very well, and then when he debated Carter on TV he stated that there was no Soviet domination of Eastern Europe and that he didn't believe that the Polish people believed they were dominated by the Soviets! Congratulations "Uncle Jimmy"!

Lesson learned: The captain was right. There are some real extremist groups in the country (not just Wisconsin). I never would have thought I would run into Nazis in uniforms or other extremist groups in America, but I have and the political ghosts of Vietnam and other conflicts are real, even today.

CHAPTER 8

Jimmy Carter, Democrat, January 1977 – January 1981

I have to admit that I had fun during President Carter's time in office, kiddingly referring to him as "Uncle Jimmy" (we weren't related). But, I wasn't as sold on him as obviously a majority of Americans must have been to elect him to office. I really think that most people were just fed up with the Republican Party at the national level with the Watergate scandal and then President Ford giving Nixon a pardon.

I thought Carter was just too naïve at the time to be President. Even though he had been a governor he came across to me, more as a farmer than a politician. I knew he had a strong religious faith and was more optimistic about the world than I was, which I felt was weakness for a president. For someone that had been a Navy officer he didn't seem to understand the dangers our country faced. Once in office, it became obvious that he didn't believe in "politics as usual". He was not one to compromise or even consider making deals with congress. This cost him a lot of support in Congress even though his party controlled both the Senate and the House.

DOMESTIC ISSUES

His second day in office, President Carter pardoned all the Vietnam War draft evaders. For many of us in the military and veterans it was a slap in the face. We didn't run out when the country needed us and many had paid the ultimate price of war. Carter made it clear that he believed we could reduce our nuclear arsenal and eventually do away with nuclear weapons in the world and abandon our military historic buildups. Nice thought but not very realistic.

Being in the USAF I understood that our people, especially SAC, were flying some old aircraft. We finally had a new bomber, the B-1, coming on line. It was state of the art and a weapon system that could effectively defend the country and wreak havoc on the USSR if necessary. Carter cancelled the program. He said that cruise missiles and the old B-52 fleet was quite capable of delivering nuclear weapons if needed. He asked for nothing from the Soviets by cancelling the program. By the time he left office, he had to begin rebuilding the military and nuclear weapons systems again.

Carter considered our dependency on foreign oil a major problem. He created the Department of Energy and decreased our dependency on foreign oil and created emergency reserves of oil and natural gas. This was a good idea but with the Iranian Revolution in 1979, high fuel prices and long lines at the gas stations reappeared and Americans just don't like long lines at the gas station or high prices. Carter paid the price during the next election.

President Carter did a few surprising things. He deregulated the airlines which ended government control over fares, routes, and entry of new airlines, and deregulated the trucking industry, and railroads. Deregulation isn't something normally associated with democrat policy. It sounded pretty good at the time, but it made the unions mad and contributed to his reelection loss to Reagan.

During his presidency we had the Three Mile Island nuclear accident which made many Americans question the wisdom of nuclear power plants for generating electricity and a federal emergency was declared over the Love Canal in Niagara Falls, NY. The Love Canal was a subdivision that had been built on top of a toxic waste dump. It was revealed that it wasn't the only location where this had happened. This is what created the "Super Fund" to clean up toxic waste dumps. The program is still in existence.

President Carter was a strong believer in human rights here at home and overseas. He knew that our judicial system was rather one-sided and appointed more Latinos and African Americans to the federal courts than any other president at that time.

Domestically not all stayed calm during his presidency. We had 10 major riots across the country. There are three that stick in my memory. July 1977 we had the New York City, blackout riot with 1000 fires and 1600 stores ransacked. In 1979, there was the Levittown gas riot. Thousands rioted in response to increased gas prices. Gas stations were damaged and cars set on fire. Around 200 people were arrested with approximately 200 rioters injured, and 44 police officers hurt. Also that year was the Greensboro, North Carolina massacre in November with a shootout between the KKK, the American Nazi Party, and Communist Workers Party. Anyone looking for a revolution?

INTERNATIONAL ISSUES

This was a trying time for the US and the International community. Historically, we still considered communism as our greatest threat. The communist were making moves in Central and South America, Africa, and the Middle East. Consequently, we backed and supported many regimes of autocrats. Sort of a hold your nose, they aren't communists philosophy.

Carter as previously stated was a strong believer in human rights here and overseas. Here in the western hemisphere he cut off financial and military aid that we had been providing to Nicaragua, El Salvador, and Chile over their human rights abuses. He worked to try to establish more democratic governments in Africa, a noble goal but not quite successful.

South Korea was a major ally to the US. We had maintained a large number of troops there since the seize fire of the Korean War. President Carter stated three months after taking office that he wanted a gradual withdraw of our forces. He felt that South Korea could build up their forces to protect themselves from North Korea. April 1978 the President announced a scheduled withdraw of

2/3 of our troops by the end of the year. North Korea must have been elated.

The Panama Canal was built in the early 1900s by treaty with the Panamanian government. Most people didn't realize that the Canal Zone wasn't a US territory. The Canal was important to us for many reasons related to national defense. We had a strong military presence to defend the canal and to also operate anywhere in Central or South America if need be. Unfortunately we treated the Canal Zone as if it was ours and ours alone. The citizens of Panama felt that we were treating them as a US possession or territory and not a sovereign nation. This lead to disagreements and even hostile reactions for many years. Efforts had been made in the '50s and '60s to come to an agreement of both countries to the administration of the canal but to no acceptable conclusion. In 1968 a government had been elected on the platform of taking back the canal and removing the US military bases. Less than 10 months later a military coup removed the elected president and a military junta took over. In 1973 General Omar Torrijos led the country. He demanded the canal be turned over to the Panamanians and US military leave by the end of the century. We faced a lot of world pressure in support of the Panamanians. The secret effort that had begun during the Ford administration to rewrite the treaty, was concluded during the Carter administration and turned the canal over to the Panamanian government. The American people felt that Carter was a weak leader that had given away the canal without any thought of American interest.

The Middle East has been a hotbed for centuries. In modern times though there has been two main issues: oil and Israel. Following the end of WWII the State of Israel was formed. We were the first nation to recognize Israel and that put us on a collision course with the rest of the Arab world. There have been many attempts to defeat Israel by the Arab nations and a state of war still technically exists between some of those nations and Israel today. While I was in the Navy in 1967 the Six-Day war broke out and Israel captured the Saini Peninsula from Egypt, half of the Golan Heights from Syria, and the West Bank from Jordan. The Arab nations held a meeting September 1967. Egypt, Syria, Jordan, Iraq, Lebanon, Algeria, Kuwait, and Sudan pledged no peace, no recognition, and no negotiation with

Israel. In 1970 after years of their militarily harassing Israel, a cease-fire was signed. Anwar Sadat became president of Egypt upon the death of Gamal Nasser. Sadat wanted peace in the Mideast but the Israelis wouldn't agree to his terms so in 1973 the Yom Kipper War or Arab-Israeli war broke out. Israel won again defeating Egypt, Syria, and the PLO. The other countries stayed away as much as they could.

The US considered Israel a "cold-war" ally. The USSR was allied with the Arabs. Neither of us wanted to get involved more than we were providing weapons for fear of "détente" being harmed and war between the two of us. So, Israel won again.

Sadat decided he wanted peace in the Mid-East for the good of his country. Despite his attempts at peace it was November 1977 before Sadat went to Israel and spoke to the Knesset. President Carter became involved as a mediator between Egypt and Israel and September 1978 invited the leaders of both countries to Camp David for secret discussions which resulted in the peace treaty between the two countries. Israel withdrew from the Sinai and Egypt recognized Israel. This was the highlight of the Carter administration.

Egypt became America's friend and ally in the Mid-East. The USSR lost their biggest asset in the Mid-East. Sadat sought peace for his people, but October 1981 he was assassinated by his own military.

The Iranian hostage situation put a damper on Carter's Mid-East success story. Iran had been a monarchy for over 2500 years. Mohammad Reza Pahlavi came to power after WWII following the abdication of his father. In 1954 the Iranian Prime Minister who had nationalized the British owned oil industry was overthrown by a coup d'état by the CIA and the United Kingdom. The Shah now had complete power. He began to build Iran into a modern country giving women suffrage, built a modern military (5th largest in the world at the time), and spent billions on building a modern industry and health care system in the country. He visualized Iran be a world leader.

One problem though, he lost the support of the clergy and the people because of corruption in the government and royal family. His secret service tortured and imprisoned any opposition. He established relationships with Israel and the US. As a matter of fact we trained his air force here in the US and sold the most up to date aircraft to him.

His opposition party was banished. It was just a matter of time before a revolt would break out. By 1978 a revolt made it untenable for him and he left in exile. He fled to Egypt where Sadat gave him protection and several other Mid-East countries. He eventually went to Mexico and wanted to come to the US for his cancer treatment. Carter didn't want him here but Henry Kissinger pressured him by refusing to indorse the Salt II agreement. Carter finally agreed because he needed Republican support for the Salt II agreement. The President was warned by the State Department that allowing the Shah to come into the country could lead to the Iranians seizing the Embassy but Carter relented to Kissinger and November 4, 1979 the US Embassy was seized and Americans were taken hostage. (By this time I had transferred to Recruiting Group Headquarters at Chanute AFB, IL). We wondered what would be done.

President Carter tried to negotiate with the Iranians but to no avail. Finally in April 1980 a rescue attempt (Operation Eagle Claw) was made. Special teams flew into Iran in a sandstorm. One chopper had a malfunction and hit a transport plane killing 18. The mission was scrubbed. Once again Carter had failed. The hostages were held for 444 days and the American people remembered. President Carter was crushed in the election.

The USSR was still the greatest threat to us. Carter and Brezhnev finally signed the Salt II agreement in June 1979. The purpose was to limit the number of nuclear weapons and development of new missile systems by both sides. However the Senate never ratified the treaty because the Soviet Union invaded Afghanistan in December and this was considered a threat to the oil supplies of the Persian Gulf and Pakistan.

The Carter Administration finally got the wake-up call. He announced sanctions on the USSR, provided aid to Pakistan and the Mujahedeen, tabled the Salt II agreement, renewed registration for the Selective Service (Draft), placed a grain embargo on the USSR, boycotted the 1980 Olympics in Moscow, and requested an increase in defense spending. So much for détente. The cold war was back on. It was my hope that the American people realized that "peace comes only through strength".

Looking back I consider President Carter one of the worst Presidents I have ever lived or served under, but I consider him a good person. I admire all that he has done since leaving office. His volunteer efforts to provide housing for the needy, his promotion of fair and free elections overseas, and his ability to live up to his faith speaks highly of him.

My opinion: Religious believes and real world politics generally don't mix very well. The world is filled with some bad actors and you have to deal from a position of strength or something you don't want to happen, will happen.

CHAPTER 9

Ronald Reagan, GOP, January 1981 - 1989

Ronald Reagan couldn't have had better timing to go against a sitting President. He asked the voters a simple question, "Are you better off now than you were four years ago?" Obviously the American public didn't think so for he trounced Carter in the election.

The morale in the country was extremely low. You couldn't watch the nightly news without seeing the Iranians burning our flag and yelling death to America. The USSR had invaded Afghanistan which scared everyone into thinking that the communist were going for the Middle Eastern oil fields. The economy was in a recession with high inflation and gasoline shortages. Despite Carter's final realization that we needed to build up the military, it was felt that we were behind the Soviets in missile and conventional war capability. The failed attempt to rescue the hostages in Iran added to this fear. Faith in the government to be able to accomplish anything was shaken. American optimism was replaced by self-absorbed worship of the consumption of material things. Even though Carter was regarded as a Christian man, a new political evangelical group founded by televangelist, Jerry Falwell, calling themselves the Moral Majority opposed him because of his stand on legalized abortion and equal rights for women. He didn't have a chance to win re-election.

Reagan on the other hand was a conservative's dream come true. I had identified him back in the 60s as someone that would be president someday. Even though for many years he was a Democrat he switched parties and gained my support. He was a staunch anti-communist. He stressed a belief in a strong military, smaller federal government, and that the American people could achieve anything. A former president of the Screen Actors Guild (a union) he had successfully served two terms as the governor of California (1967 to 1975). He supported Senator Barry Goldwater when Goldwater ran for president. He was very vocal about his religious believes and that contributed to his popularity with the Republican Party and the American people.

The Republican Party took control of the Senate for the next six years, but the Democrats maintained control of the House.

THE GREAT COMMUNICATOR?

I have to admit that I thought Reagan did a tremendous job talking to the American people. The truth is he was an actor that knew how to play to his audience. He had a great sense of humor and had no problem laughing at himself and I think that endured him to the people and covered up a lot of mistakes he made. He said one thing though that really bothered me ... "government is not the solution to our problems; **government is the problem**". I think many may have taken that to heart and has contributed to a lot of what is going on in the country today.

AMERICA TALKS AND ACTS TOUGH

When Reagan took office he was credited with the release of the hostages in Iran. The general believe was that it happened because of his strong stance during the election about building back up America's military power. It was later revealed that there was a trade of weapons to the Iranians for the release.

During his first month in office, in support of his belief in downsizing the federal government he put a freeze on federal hiring. When he held his first news conference he called out the Soviets saying they would commit any crime, lie, and cheat to achieve their goals of communist domination of the world.

As for me I was transferred again this time to Oklahoma as a Squadron Recruiter Trainer and Science and Engineer Officer Recruiter on the University of Oklahoma campus. Times were changing and we were ready for America to be back.

Three months into his Presidency, he was shot in an assassination attempt. I was stunned. In my lifetime we had President Kennedy, Martin Luther King, and Robert Kennedy, assassinated, two assassination attempts on President Ford, and now an attempt on President Reagan. I wondered is this what America is coming to? Fortunately he survived, but while in the hospital it was discovered to be a very serious wounding. Actor that he was, he played it up like nothing serious had happened and appeared at his hospital window to wave to the press and public. What we didn't know at the time was that his wife, Nancy Reagan turned to an astrologist to protect her husband and influence decisions he made from that point onward. Later in his presidency there was some concern that maybe his mental facilities were breaking down.

Reagan had a lot of hardliners in his cabinet. More of a hands off leader, he leaned heavily on his advisors and generally went along with what they wanted and recommended. We went into a military build-up that basically doubled the DOD budget. He reinstated the B-1 bomber program and the neutron bomb program, along with an increase of nuclear weapons, cruise missiles, and the B-2 stealth bomber. Despite all this, following the assassination attempt he believed that God had saved him to reduce the threat of nuclear war. Rather contradictory but peace through strength was the plan.

Reagan was really concerned about communism expanding in the world. He was particularly concerned about Central America, South America, and Africa. Sword rattling by both sides was quite common. June of 1982 he visited West Berlin where he was met by demonstrators calling him a fascist, go home, and calling for his assassination. Mind boggling.

August of 1982 we deployed US Marines along with French forces to Lebanon as part of a Peacekeeping Force, following the invasion of that country by Israel and with civil war breaking out. We had backed the Israelis with weapons and logistics support. There would be a price to be paid. Iran was backing the forces opposing Israel.

The following year he gave his famous "Evil Empire" speech to the National Association of Evangelicals. He also announced the "Star Wars" program. We were going to militarize space with laser weapons. That made my job more interesting since I recruited engineers. I took groups of engineer students to many of our research and development labs for tours. I learned more about lasers than I would have ever guessed. I had a recruiting film titled Air Force 21st Century that covered everything from projected space craft being developed, to lasers shooting down aircraft, and kids playing computer games that would develop the future skills needed to fly aircraft. It was a powerful tool that got me interviews on television and radio and the Top Engineer Recruiter award.

That same year in October we invaded Grenada. US troops fought against Cuban military and communist forces. The operation ended two months later and the American public finally took a real positive outlook on our military. It was our first public victory since Vietnam, but at the same time the USMC peacekeepers in their Beirut barracks were attacked by a suicide bomber. Hundreds of marines were killed. Reagan pulled our forces out. Personally as a military member, I was shocked that one incident would end our involvement.

The following month during a NATO exercise (Reforger), we came close to nuclear war with the Soviet Union. I encourage you to read **Able Archer 83**, edited by Nate Jones. Able Archer 83 was a highly classified operation that simulated the use of nuclear weapons against the Soviets. It has just recently been declassified and through the Freedom of Information Act, and made public.

President Reagan never believed that the US would strike first against the USSR and believed that the Soviets thought the same. However, Reagan's rhetoric about the communist threat and public speeches about building our offensive capabilities, including forward deployment of Pershing II missiles in Europe, Star Wars talk and our actions in Lebanon and Grenada scared the hell out of the Soviets. During the NATO exercise they picked up on the message traffic between our forces and thought they were real preparations for a first strike. They moved their nuclear forces forward, armed their planes with nukes and was ready to launch. It was a hair trigger event. When the exercise was over and the Soviets were convinced we weren't going to attack them, calm returned. When Reagan was briefed as to what had happened he was shocked and it scared the hell out of him. It was time to get serious about negotiating with the Soviets. He decided that it was time to drop the threat speeches and begin talking about disarmament.

This wouldn't be the last time we came close to accidently going to nuclear war during his administration. There were computer foul ups on both sides that indicated the other side had launched ICBMS. If cooler heads hadn't prevailed we would be living in a nuclear wasteland as the response would be launching in retaliation while still able to do so.

If all this isn't bad enough, August of 1984, Reagan's sense of humor caused an uproar. He didn't realize that he was on an open microphone at an event when he jokingly said that we would be bombing Russia in 5 minutes! I started wondering if he knew what he was doing. It was an election year. Reagan won 49 out of 50 states defeating former Vice-President Mondale.

As 1986 rolled around we lost the space shuttle Challenger. The country was in shock and President Reagan gave a heart-warming speech to the country that picked up the moral.

April 1986 we bombed Libya in retaliation of a nightclub bombing in West Berlin that killed and injured several US military personnel. No talk just action. Don't mess with us.

By October a real effort was being made to ban all ballistic missiles and reduce the chance of nuclear war. The Soviets really wanted to end the threat. Reagan met with Gorbachev in Iceland but the talks collapsed over the Star Wars initiative. The chance for maybe real peace fell apart. The next month the Iran-Contra Affair came to light. We were illegally diverting money from the sale of weapons to Iran to the Contra rebels in Nicaragua which was prohibited by congress. Reagan came close to being impeached over the affair. It was probably his televised speech to the American people that saved him.

In 1987 the Democrats took back the Senate and controlled both houses of congress again. Also in

1987 the Intermediate Range Nuclear Forces Treaty with the USSR would be signed but 1988 before finalization of the INF treaty would be signed.

As the Berlin Wall came down and the USSR started allowing Eastern Block satellite countries out from under their thumb, everyone was saying the cold war is over! I didn't believe it. You just don't overnight change your thinking, especially in politics. Russia, as we now know it, had been under an autocratic government, communist control, for too many years. I knew in my heart there would be someone wanting things as they had been, absolute power vested in one leader or a small group of people. They just had to find a way to get back in control. Unfortunately it seems I was right.

THE ECONOMICS OF THE "ME FIRST GENERATION"

The buildup of the military led to more jobs but the tax cuts led to more borrowing of money to run the government and inflation. At the same time domestic cuts in spending led to more poverty for those at the lower levels of income.

During his eight years as President we had a 92 month boom. He never submitted a balanced budget and we engaged in high deficit spending. The federal debt ballooned from $994 billion to $2.9 trillion. Sooner or later something had to give.

When I transferred to Oklahoma the oil boom was going on. Housing was in a shortage. People were coming into the state to work in the oil fields and money was being spent like it was going out of style. At Lake Hefner, one of the Oklahoma City's reservoirs and parks, people had established a tent city just to have a place to live.

As the recruiter trainer for the squadron I took a new recruiter to one of his high schools to demonstrate how you approach the school administration and explain that the Air Force wanted their students to stay in school and graduate and then join the Air Force. When we got to the school the parking lot was filled with almost nothing but new cars. The principal pointed out that the cars belonged to the students not the faculty. He was having a hard time getting the students to stay in school rather than working in the oil patch and if we could get them to finish their education, we could have all the students!

In paradox to the wealth being made in the oil fields, downtown Oklahoma City left a lot to be desired. Many of the older buildings were boarded up and the number of homeless street people was mind boggling. Even if you were working trying to find a place to live was a challenge. People were filling up hotel rooms renting them by the month. It was like the gold rush days. It seemed like there was a strip club on every corner willing to take your money. Liquor was by the wink, as the bars were bottle clubs where you provided the booze and then got charged to drink out of your own bottle. It was crazy. I never saw so many people wearing gold jewelry, driving new vehicles, and spending money like a drunken sailor. Interest rates for a home loan ran from 16% to 18%. People were using credit for everything and thought nothing of it. You could go to your mailbox and find that you had a new credit card that you didn't apply for, waiting for you and all you had to do was start using it. Along with crazy personal economics, drugs, crime, and murders were increasing.

Reagan once said that, "Unemployment is a pre-paid vacation for freeloaders". Then it happened.

In 1982 the oil boom busted. Penn Square bank in Oklahoma City closed and people lost almost all their money. The effect was International. The Savings and Loan crisis caused by Junk Bonds occurred. The economy plummeted, families lost their oil businesses, their jobs, their homes, and all they had accumulated. Home values dropped up to 66% overnight. Bankruptcies became quite common. There were many people now filing for unemployment and I don't think they were "freeloaders". If you have never seen the 1987 movie, Wall Street, starring Michael Douglas and Charlie Sheen, watch it as it tells the story of what was going on and the mindset that fueled the "Me First" attitude and economic collapse.

Following all this, in Oklahoma we had a former governor indicted for bribery and several county commissioners prosecuted for bribery. The hard working people were just a little upset with what was going on.

NEW CHALLENGES

Eventually I would join the Engineering and Science Officer recruiting team. I was responsible for the colleges and universities in Oklahoma. My office was located in the student union of the University of Oklahoma. It was a great assignment and a lot of fun, but there were some things going on I found interesting. We still had a lot of Iranian students attending college here. In an attempt to keep from being sent back to Iran they would finish one year at one school and then transfer to another. How they got away with that I will never know but there was plenty of hatred against the Iranian students. I also had a case where apparently the Air Force Office of Special Investigations (AFOSI) notified our squadron of a possible bombing attack against us. We were told to check our vehicles for any wires that didn't look right before getting in them and to not leave our government cars at the office. Sure enough, I found a wire under my vehicle that didn't look right. Contacting my superiors I was told not to enter the vehicle until either someone from EOD or the bomb squad checked it out. After about six hours and with no one showing up, I got in the vehicle and drove away. No bomb.

After two years recruiting officers, I went back to my old job as the Squadron Trainer. Graduating from the Non-Commissioned Officer Academy I was promoted to Master Sergeant. Another NCO who had just been promoted to Master Sergeant came up to me and said we needed to take the Senior NCO Academy so we could get promoted to Senior Master Sergeant. Looking at him I said, "Don't you think you should learn how to become a good Master Sergeant before worrying about your next promotion?" He looked at me like I was crazy. Even in the Air Force we had people who were part of the "Me First" crowd.

At the time I was thinking about leaving recruiting duty and returning to the mainstream Air Force and had orders to the AWACS (Airborne Warning and Control) unit on Tinker AFB. My recruiting commander wanted to know why and I told him that I was looking for more responsibility. He offered me a position as Flight Supervisor of Recruiters in Oklahoma City. All I had to do was turn down my orders and stay with the squadron. I did so. Three weeks later he told me that I was taking over one of our flights in Missouri and one of the people from there would be the Flight Supervisor in Oklahoma City. So much for trusting that guy. It turned out to be a good move as we became the number one flight in the squadron and the squadron commander and some members of his staff (including the squadron superintendent) were replaced. Recruiting became challenging again.

My office was located in Joplin, Missouri. My flight covered SW Missouri, SE Kansas, and part of NE Oklahoma, but mainly Missouri. One thing that I learned right away was that SW Missouri was a very different place. People were very open about their prejudice against minorities. Also, there were some very bad groups of militias located there. It turned out that about 20 miles from where I lived there was a militia training camp. It also became obvious to me that the poverty level was higher in my area. People working at one of the poultry processing plants made minimum wage and when they were getting to the point of qualifying for company benefits they got laid off and when they were called back to work had to start all over again to qualify for the benefit program.

As Reagan left office, I left recruiting duty and finally transferred back to Oklahoma and joined the 963rd Airborne Warning and Control Squadron, at Tinker AFB. The Democrats controlled both houses of congress and George H.W. Bush was elected President.

My opinion: Nothing is simply black or white. Government isn't always the problem but the people in power can be a problem. Reagan had some real hardliners giving him advice that almost got us into trouble. President Teddy Roosevelt said, "Speak softly, but carry a big stick". We came close to nuclear war several times because we didn't speak softly and joked about going to war. I also started feeling that we were looking at the military options to solve our problems too readily. Was it to distract from our domestic problems? It is also important to maintain fiscal responsibility. The national debt soared and our economy had crashed and burned with a lot of people paying the price. What happened to the GOP and fiscal responsibility?

CHAPTER 10

George H. W. Bush, GOP January 1989 - 1993

I felt pretty good about George H.W. Bush being elected president. I voted for him. He had an excellent background in business and politics for the job. A WWII Navy pilot that had been shot down in combat, a successful oilman, a congressman, former Ambassador to the UN, Chief Liaison to China, former Director of the CIA and eight years as Vice-President under Ronald Reagan, Michael Dukakis didn't have a chance against him. He would be the last veteran of WWII to serve as President. He was a conservative and his stance on "no new taxes" appealed to the public in general. Unfortunately his promise couldn't be fulfilled due to a soaring budget deficit. This would come to haunt him later.

President Bush was more of an international leader than a domestic leader. He accomplished many important things during this period such as the end of the Cold War and reducing nuclear weapons of the US and USSR after signing a mutual nonaggression pact with Soviet leader Mikhail Gorbachev. Communism in Eastern

Europe and the USSR fell, and Germany was reunified. Many people thought that Russia would now come around to our way of thinking. Personally, I didn't buy that Russia was now going to be our friend. I believed the Russian people would want an end to the cold war and communism but not the people in government.

Bush wasn't as flamboyant as Ronald Regan but he was steady. He understood that we had a lot of problems such as homelessness, crime, and drug addiction in our country. He thought volunteerism and community action groups were the answer, especially since the Democrats controlled both houses of congress and he inherited a federal debt of $2.8 trillion dollars and a lack of revenues to do anything about our domestic problems. He had to back-off on his pledge about no new taxes. Following a brief government shutdown as a result of vetoing a congressional budget submitted to him, he did reach a compromise with congress that reduced government spending and raised taxes. His conservative base began to turn against him.

DOMESTIC CHALLENGES FOR THE COUNTRY

The Savings and Loan industry was collapsing do to deregulation. The economy was heading downward. Bush sold congress on a plan to save the industry costing the taxpayers $100 billion dollars. Once again the conservative base wasn't happy but it saved the industry, the real estate market, and other industries.

Another win for the country was the Americans with Disabilities Act forbidding discrimination by employers against the disabled, provided access to businesses, public buildings and telecommunications, giving the disabled more independence. I was surprised that many felt this was an intrusion by the federal government into the private sector. I thought that it was a necessary and humane thing to do as it enabled many disable people to enjoy and take advantage of things that the rest of us just took for granted.

Another domestic win was the amendments to the Clean Air Act. Once again many conservatives opposed this but the environmental disaster of the Exxon Valdez spilling more than 10 million gallons of oil in Alaska changed a lot of minds. Now attention could be focused on reducing urban smog, acid rain, and industrial emissions of toxic chemicals. Unfortunately these problems are still with us today and appear to be growing.

Some problems never seem to get better and race relations is one of the biggest that still divides our country. On March 3, 1991, in Los Angeles, an individual named Rodney King led police on a high speed chase. He was finally stopped, arrested for DWI, but the arresting officers beat him during the arrest. It was all caught on camera and televised nationwide. The arresting officers were charged but in April of 1992 were acquitted triggering riots. Over 50 people were killed, around 2000 injured, and 9600 were arrested for rioting, looting, and arson. There was over $1 billion dollars in property damage. Watching all this on television made LA and other cities look like a war zone.

GOING FROM "COLD WAR" TO HOT WAR

I was still in the USAF when Bush was elected. After 13 years with Recruiting Service I was returning to my primary skill in the Air Force. Joining the 963rd Airborne Warning and Control Squadron I was excited to be back with a flying unit. After a few months in the squadron I became the First Sergeant for the squadron. I was one of the few First Sergeants that actually flew with a few crews on missions. My people were absolutely professional and knew their jobs. Initially it was mainly training missions that we were on but eventually we supported the drug interdiction program. I really felt that we were doing something extremely important for our country and took great pride in it. When we rotated out and another squadron took on the mission it was back to supporting training missions and NATO missions.

I flew with a crew to Great Briton for a training exercise there. While we were there Saddam was preparing to invade Kuwait. It appeared that war could be imminent. Since we were the only E-3 forward deployed, we thought for sure we would deploy from Great Britain but were ordered home.

Why did we get involved? The Mid-East has always been a trouble spot mostly over religious reasons, but it was a different case this time. About 65% of the oil production in the world came from the region. The Iraqi regime was a threat to Saudi Arabia and the other oil producing nations in the region. Even though we had supported the Iraqis in their conflict with Iran Saddam's invasion of Kuwait was a step too far.

Thirty-five nations joined the coalition to stop them. Whoever controlled the oil controlled the region and would be a strong influencer in world politics. Democracy had nothing to do with it.

"Shock and Awe" was the war plan and it worked. I was surprised that it ended so quickly and I think most of America was surprised. Our military leadership didn't want another Vietnam. I remember though one of the airman in the squadron asked me what I thought and my reply was "if we don't go to Baghdad and finish this, my kids will fight here one day". Both of my sons served in the second Gulf War.

Unlike Vietnam, the military was welcomed back as heroes. Parades were scheduled across the country. Many of the Vietnam vets wanted to make sure that the troops weren't treated like they were during their war. Some though had a little heartburn. I had a friend with a bumper sticker that read "I am not a Desert Storm Hero, just a Vietnam Vet". Sometimes the hurt just never goes away.

There were some pluses and minuses to the war and how quickly it was "won". It showed the world how with the right leadership maybe the U.S. was not someone you wanted to mess with.

We had a highly trained and motivated military and our leaders knew how to put together a coalition to stand up to aggression. The downside is that it led some of our leaders and future leaders to believe that all we had to do internationally was send our military to kick butt for a few days to settle any disputes. In the future I would question why politicians ran for the title of Commander-in-Chief, rather than President of the United States. Stop and think about that.

I decided that 1991 would be my last year in the military and retired January 1, 1992. After 26yrs of service it was time to move on.

Becoming a civilian again wasn't difficult but deciding what I would do was up in the air. With a family with young kids I knew I needed a career that would allow me to at least earn what I did on active duty. I decided to get a real estate license and remain in Oklahoma. I was fortunate to be rather successful with Century 21 and made decent money and contacts.

It was during this time frame that President George H.W. Bush was running for another term as president. He had a strong contender for the nomination in Pat Buchanan but defeated him. The real threat to re-election appeared to be Ross

Perot with some guy named Bill Clinton the candidate for the Democrat party. I thought Bush would be a shoe-in with the winning of the Gulf War as part of his credentials, but something happened. As the election drew closer, it was almost like he didn't care if re-elected or not. Clinton won. I was shocked and only met one person that admitted they had voted for him.

My opinion: I was proud to have served my country during this time frame and was elated to see how the country responded to the military in our victory over Iraq. Bush had done an excellent job in getting a coalition together to get the job done. I was concerned that we didn't finish the mission at the time and feared that we would be back again sometime in the future. I was also concerned that because the war had ended so quickly that people would think that all future conflicts would go the same way and that the military option would be used all too often without thinking things through and gathering the facts before taking action. Unfortunately history proved me right.

CHAPTER 11

Bill Clinton, Democrat, January 1993 - 2001

When Clinton was elected President, I really felt that the country was going to be in serious trouble. We already had financial problems with the national debt and we had some extreme religious groups that thought the world was coming to an end and other extremist thought the government was going to take their guns away. The Ruby Ridge incident in 1992 was a good example that made the news at the time. It ended in a big shootout with US Marshalls and the FBI and a former Green Beret up in Idaho. Down in Axtell, TX we had another group called the Branch Davidians whose leader thought he was Christ and he and his followers were armed to the teeth and ready to take on the government. February 1993 was the start of a 51 day siege by federal and state law enforcement when the ATF attempted to serve a search warrant for illegal weapons. A gunfight erupted killing four government agents and six Davidians. It ended April 19th with the facility burning down during a tear gas attack by the FBI. Seventy-six Davidians including 25 children and two pregnant women died. It reminded me of the Jonestown Massacre of 1978, when 900 plus people members of the People's Temple in Guyana committed suicide and killed Congressman Leo Ryan when he visited. They claimed the government was coming after them. It was propaganda that people fell for either through mind-control or behavior modification. I don't know which.

Clinton's newly appointed Attorney General, Janet Reno would catch a lot of criticism over the Waco attack. Some of us would pay more dearly later.

I didn't know much about Clinton but I had friends in Arkansas that said he had a bad reputation as governor for fooling around with women. I also knew that he had avoided the draft and serving in the military during the Vietnam War. I pictured him as part of the "me generation" and probably couldn't be trusted. He had Al Gore as his Vice-President, another southerner from Tennessee. My initial thought was here we go again with people that probably don't know the civil war is over.

None of the candidates for President seem to be overwhelmingly popular. Clinton had 43%, Bush 37%, and Perot 19% of the popular vote. I often wondered what the results would have been if Perot hadn't run. The Electoral College was the biggest split. Clinton had 370, Bush with 168, and Perot was zero.

GOOD AND BAD RESULTS

President Clinton didn't get off to a very good start. He had campaigned on several issues that were doomed to failure. His promise to end discrimination against Gays and Lesbians in the military – failed. Not even Colin Powell would support that. They did compromise with "Don't Ask and Don't Tell" policy which I had no problem with.

Clinton had trouble with some nominees for Attorney General even though the Democrats controlled House and Senate during his first two years in office. Two nominees had to withdraw from consideration due to questioning about their domestic help. He ran on the idea of campaign finance reform and that failed. That was something I could support but still hasn't happened and I doubt it ever will and he pushed for Universal Healthcare and failed. It would be two more administrations before anything resembling that would happen.

Immediately it seemed that the Clinton administration was going to have problems. An investigation into his and his wife's involvement with Whitewater a real estate investment deal back in Arkansas came up. Ken Starr was appointed as special investigator and made life pretty miserable for Clinton for both terms of office. He ended up expanding the investigation after spending $50 million and finding no conclusive evidence of any wrongdoing, the investigation of the President turned to Clinton's extra-curricular activities with women. This led to Clinton's impeachment for committing perjury and obstruction of justice in the Monica Lewinsky case. He was found not guilty in the Senate trial and became only the second president to ever be impeached. He would have been the third if Nixon hadn't resigned to avoid impeachment. The Republican Party controlled both the House and Senate when this occurred. I couldn't believe that in my lifetime two presidents faced impeachment. What was going on in government to think that could even happen?

Clinton's real problem was Newt Gingrich, the Republican Speaker of the House. Gingrich was a real thorn in the side. He was primarily the one responsible for the polarization of American politics and partisan prejudice that still haunts our political system today. Even though he pushed for Clinton's impeachment for fooling around with Lewinsky, it eventually came to light that Gingrich was guilty of the same thing with a woman in her 20s. He was quick to accuse people of things that quite often he was found to be doing himself. Sort of the pot calling the kettle black.

President Clinton did succeed in some areas that made me wonder if he was really a Republican rather than a Democrat. He implemented welfare reform that required work requirements and time limitations on receiving welfare. As a conservative I always believed you should offer a helping hand to people but they need to also help themselves. He made it easier for Americans to register to vote with the Motor Voter Registration Act which allowed you register to vote when obtaining your driver's license. Once again as a Republican I believe that every citizen has a right to vote and we should do whatever we can to insure every citizen gets a chance to exercise that right. His administration passed the Deficit Reduction Act without any Republican votes to slash the deficit in half. This alone helped the Medicare Trust Fund and turned what had been the country's largest deficit in history into the largest surplus of funds. Also, even though negotiations had begun during the Bush Administration, the North American Free Trade Agreement (NAFTA) passed which created the world's largest free trade zone.

For those of us that were fed up with crime, the implementation of the Crime Bill which included the "three strikes and you're out" provision was passed. Clinton also succeeded in gaining funding for local governments to hire 100,000 police officers and despite differences in opinion with many of my fellow gun owners, the Assault Weapons Ban was passed. That law would eventually expire but overall gun violence did drop while in effect. I love to shoot and hunt, but I never could understand why a large capacity, semi-automatic rifle that could be converted to full automatic, was necessary for deer hunting.

In 1996 Clinton ran for re-election against one of my heroes, Senator Bob Dole of Kansas. He beat Senator Dole with 379 electoral votes to 159 for Dole. The popular vote was 49.2% for Clinton and 40.7% for Dole. It was the first time in history, since FDR that a Democrat President got re-elected.

By the time he left office in 2001, with a Republican majority in the House and Senate for the final six years of his presidency we had the longest economic expansion in American history, highest home ownership, lowest unemployment in 30 years, lowest crime rate is 26 years, smallest welfare rolls in 32 years, lowest poverty rate in 20 years, paid off $360 billion of the national debt, and had the lowest government spending in three decades. (Info provided by https://clintonwhitehouse5.archives.gov/WH/...)

I think this shows that it is possible to work in a bi-partisan way and serve for the good of the public even if you don't like the person in office.

INTERNATIONAL TROUBLES

December 9, 1992, before he left office, President Bush had authorized deployment of 25,000 troops to Somali to support a United Nations effort. This was supposed to be a humanitarian effort to help the starving people in a country being ravaged civil war. In June of 1993, President Clinton reduced the number of US troops to 1200. There were troops there from 28 countries. Instead of providing humanitarian relief, we ended up battling militia. The UN wanted one of the leaders of the rebellion captured and brought to trial because 24 Pakistani soldiers had been killed. August of 1993, 400 special operation troops were sent to get the job done. October 3, 1993 the seventh attempt to capture the individual was made. US Special Operations personnel entered Mogadishu. Two helicopters supporting the effort were shot down. Two pilots were hacked to death and their mutilated bodies were dragged through the streets. The battle of Mogadishu or "Black Hawk Down" began. All this was seen on television news. We had 18 US soldiers killed and 84 wounded. A friend of mine that was an Army Sergeant Major and there, said it was the worst fighting he had ever been involved in. Following the battle, President Clinton removed our troops.

Some success towards ending hostilities in the world succeeded. In 1994 the Clinton Administration helped with the reinstatement of Haiti's elected President who had been ousted during a coup in 1991. In 1995 the administration led the Dayton Accords ending the war in Bosnia. A peace accord was brokered in 1998 in Northern Ireland and that year we launched air attacks against Iraqi NBC weapons programs. In 1999 we led a NATO alliance in a 79 day air war in Kosovo that defeated Serb forces committing ethnic cleansing.

MORE TROUBLE ON THE HOME FRONT

As 1995 rolled around I was thinking about making a career change. A friend of mine mentioned that the insurance company he represented was wanting to start a military division and asked if I would least ways consider talking to his manager about joining the team. It was the morning of April 19, when we met at his office. Stepping outside for a smoke break we heard a loud noise and felt a concussion. I looked at my friend who was retired Air Force and said it sounded like a 500lb bomb had gone off. We went back inside and they had a television set turned on. It was announced that there had been an explosion in downtown Oklahoma City. Possibly a natural gas line had exploded. It wasn't a gas line but a bomb. It was a terrorist attack against the Alfred P. Murrah Federal Building. No one would have ever expected such a thing to happen here. Bombings and terrorist attacks happened in other countries. We had 168 people killed in the explosion including children in a daycare center. Extensive damage occurred to buildings surround the site.

Once it was known that it wasn't an accident but a bombing the question was who did it? Some thought that it might have been Iraqis seeking revenge over the war or some other radical Islamic group. The anger was on the street and if you looked like an Arab, people wondered about you.

It wasn't a foreign group that attacked the building but **two American extremist with ties to White Supremacists groups and right-wing terrorist.** Timothy McVeigh and Terry Nichols would eventually be captured and convicted for the attack. They had met each other in 1988 while serving in the Army. Both of them were upset with the government response to the Ruby Ridge and Waco events and sought revenge. McVeigh was put to death and Nichols is still in prison.

President Clinton came to Oklahoma City and grieved with the rest of us. In April of 1996 he signed the Anti-terrorism and Effective Death Penalty Act to combat terrorism at home and abroad giving the Federal government broad jurisdiction to prosecute terrorist.

Following the attack against the Murrah Building I did change careers. I was contacted by my old boss from Air Force Recruiting. He wanted to know if I still knew how to recruit and if I could still talk Navy from my early days in the USN. I accepted the position as an the International Recruiter for the Royal Saudi Navy contract Lear-Siegler, Inc (LSI) had with the Saudi government. It was a dream job working with Navy veterans placing them in positions based on their career fields in the Navy. I would be travelling all over the country visiting Navy bases and working job fairs. The smoke was still in the air from the bombing when I started work there.

Two years later May 3, 1999, the Oklahoma City area suffered another disaster. An F5 tornado struck. I lived in Del City, a small town located next to Tinker AFB. It had been 50 years since a tornado had touched down there. My oldest son and I were at the fitness center on treadmills and watching the TV. It was sunny outside but severe weather was building up to the southwest. As we are watching news it was evident that the storms and tornados were moving northeast up the toll road in our direction. I decided we should head home. As the skies darkened I grilled some burgers on the patio. We went inside to eat and tried to track down where my youngest son was at. The sirens went off. Tornado! We didn't have a storm shelter and so went to an enclosed closet.

The house shook and the roar of the tornado was just like a train. After it passed we came out of the closet expecting the worst. The walls were still standing and the roof was on the house. Out in the front and back yard, 2X4s were stuck in the ground all around the house, debris from neighbors. We hadn't been touched. I can't say that for many of my neighbors. My youngest son came home and both boys immediately went out to help others. That was the scene all around us. The next morning the devastation was even clearer, and the response from the people was amazing. Everyone came to each other's aid. Your politics, your race, nothing matters but citizens helping each other. That's America.

THE BIG DISASTER THAT DIDN'T HAPPEN

The 20th century was coming to an end and America went into a panic. The conspiracy and disaster rumors were flowing. Even the real news media was covering the stories. All of our computer systems were going to crash! Why? None of the computers would be able to read the year 2000. Everything would fall apart. All systems would fail. The economy would be a disaster, power systems would go down along with communications. There would be riots in the streets and the government would be unable to do anything about it.

Armageddon was here. Only true survivalist would make it. Sound crazy? Yep, but there were a lot of people that believed it.

Maybe there was something to it. I know a lot of companies had their IT people making sure their systems were going to be okay.

It was a time when I knew people who started building hidden shelters and stocking up on food and ammunition. I worked with one person that had bought land in Arkansas and actually had a hidden in-ground hide-away built. He also claimed to have a .50 caliber machine gun emplacement to protect his property. No telling how much money he had invested in building his "secure" hideaway. Just days before the start of the New Year and the 21st century he was inviting women from work to join him promising that he would protect them from the forthcoming disaster. As far as I know, no one took him up on his offer. January 1st came and went and nothing had changed.

November 2000 was another Presidential election. Clinton couldn't run but his Vice-

President Al Gore could. His opponent was George W. Bush, son of the former President.

My opinion: The country didn't fall apart during the Clinton years, but because of what was going on in congress with the polarizing politics and partisan prejudice, we were heading to trouble. The attitude seemed to be "kill and slander" the opposition, and build fear into the public about anyone that thought different than you.

CHAPTER 12

George W. Bush, GOP, January 2001 - 2009

The 2000 Republican primary was a real disappointment to me. I was for John McCain. I felt he really got a raw deal from the party. Despite my misgivings the party selected George W. Bush, son of the former president, former governor of Texas, a questionable member of the Texas Air National Guard, and someone that didn't strike me as being that bright. I was really concerned when Bush selected Dick Chaney as his running mate. Chaney was the person that was supposed to be in charge of finding a running mate for Bush. After screening many potentials, including the governor of Oklahoma a man I knew and supported, no one measured up. Amazingly no one fit the bill except him. Duh! My first thought was that if Bush wins, who is really going to be running things?

The Democrats had selected Vice-president Al Gore as their candidate. He came across sharper than Bush, but he had a stigma associated with President Clinton's problems and despite his best efforts to distance himself from Clinton it didn't work.

This presidential election made me questioned what was happening in our political system. The election was really, really close. The initial returns showed Gore had won the popular vote with over half a million. When 85% of the vote was counted it showed Bush was the leader. The problem was neither candidate had the 270 Electoral College votes needed to win. The key to the election was Florida and their 25 electoral votes. Bush was declared the winner of Florida. Initially Gore conceded but when Florida did their mandatory recount of machine casted votes, Bush only lead by 327 votes out of approximately 6 million cast. Gore retracted his concession. Apparently, the cards used for voting with machines had a problem. Voters had to punch the voting card to be read by the machine. Many of the cards had what was called hanging chads (not fully punched out) or dimples where they may have been punched but didn't go through. An audit was ordered and a recount by the Florida Supreme Court. The Republicans appealed the election to the US Supreme Court saying that the recount couldn't be completed by the required 18 December deadline. The country was in an uproar. How did Florida, whose governor was the brother of the Republican candidate, end up deciding the election? There were suspicions that maybe some hanky-panky was going on. **After weeks of challenges by both sides the Supreme Court for the first time in our history, selected the president. The US Supreme Court voted in a 5 to 4 decision along party lines to award the election to Bush.** Bush got 271 electoral votes (1 more than needed to win) to Gore's 266 (one Gore electoral voter didn't vote).

The Democrats had control of the Senate during the first two years of Bush's presidency and during the last two years of his eight, would control both houses.

TURBULENT YEARS

Bush's presidency had some real problems. He had inherited an economy and surplus budget that could possibly pay off the national debt, instead he pushed for a $1.3 trillion tax cut. He believed that any surplus should go back to the people and businesses. Sounds good, but if you are ever going to get out of debt you won't do it cutting your resources unless you find a way to cut your spending to offset the loss of income. Then it got worse.

I was still working for LSI recruiting people for all the government contracts we supported. It was fall of 2001, September 11th. I went into the office and noticed that one of the Vice-Presidents had a television turned on and a crowd was around it. The story was that an airplane had crashed into one of the towers of the World Trade Center. At first we thought it must have been a private aircraft. After all years ago a plane had crashed into the Empire State Building. As we watched it became clear that it was an airliner. As the story continued and we saw the smoke coming from the building, another plane appeared on screen and it too crashed into the building. This was no accident. Something was going on! It didn't take long for it to sink in that we were under attack by someone!

Immediately the VP called all the directors and managers into his office. All of us were retired military and it was evident that we would probably need to gear up for a fight somewhere and since we provided maintenance and support to all branches of DOD that we would be getting a call.

Two more planes would go down. One striking the Pentagon and another crashing in a field in

Pennsylvania. It was a high-jacking by some terrorist group but who? Who was behind it?

The country was in turmoil. We needed leadership and surprisingly enough, we had it. President Bush didn't hesitate to step up. He went to New York City where they were digging out the survivors and bodies of those lost. Standing on the rubble with first responders he said, "I hear you. The rest of the world hears you, and the people who knocked these buildings down will hear from all of us!" I couldn't have been prouder of him. Maybe this guy will be a good President after all.

It took about a week and we were told that AL Qaeda, under the leadership of Osama bin Laden, was behind the attack. He and the majority of the terrorist in the attack, were Saudis. Bin Laden was in exile in Afghanistan, which was under control of the Taliban. On September 20th, Bush told the Taliban to hand over the terrorist or share their fate. They didn't comply and October 7th the bombing of Afghanistan began. We invaded the country with Special Operations personnel and by December the Pentagon said the Taliban had been defeated. Well another short war. Really? No, bin Laden was still alive and the Taliban would regroup and the war would continue. We would get distracted with an invasion of Iraq (again) and it would be May 2011 under a different administration that bin Laden would be killed and 2021 before we would pull completely out of Afghanistan.

THE WAR AT HOME

The 9/11 attack caught America off guard. Questions were being asked how it could have even happened. What was the NSA, CIA, and FBI doing? Were they sleeping on the job or what? There had really been a breakdown in communications between our various intelligence agencies. As good as they were at what they do, they didn't always share with each other what they knew. This led to the creation of the Department of Homeland Security. It also led to some administration programs such as the President's Surveillance Program which allowed listening in on American's phone conversations and surveillance of their email accounts without a warrant. This was a violation of the Foreign Intelligence Surveillance Act. (In 2006 a federal judge ruled the NSA surveillance program was unconstitutional. His ruling was later vacated by a US Court of Appeals but the US Attorney General said the President wouldn't reauthorize the program and it would be subject to judicial oversight.) Muslim and Arab Americans were targeted by the government and came under suspicion by their neighbors. Some were taken into custody and the normal rights of these Americans were ignored. I understood the emotions at the time, but it hit me like a warning sign of things that could possibly come. The average American apparently didn't think much of these questionable actions as Bush's approval rating was at 90%.

At the same time we had the conspiracy people starting the story that actually the attack on 9/11 was a "false-flag" operation by our government led by the intelligence community and others stating that the attack hadn't happened. Yeah we didn't land on the moon either!

President Bush declared a "War on Terror" and when he delivered his state of the union to congress in January, declared an "Axis of Evil" identifying North Korea, Iran, and Iraq threaten world peace and that **the administration had the right and intention of waging preemptive war or preventive war.** Where in the hell did that come from? Only congress can declare war, right?

Bush really didn't have any international experience. He relied heavily on his vice-president and team for guidance. I believe this too led to many of our future problems and actions.

THE BIG LIE LEADING TO EXPANDED WAR

About mid-year of 2002 supposedly the CIA had reports that Saddam Hussein had re-started his weapons of mass destruction program. There have been many questions as to whether the reports were true or if the administration (primarily Vice-President Chaney) was leaning on the CIA to make such an allegation as a reason to go war against Iraq. Why would the administration do that? One theory was that Saddam was behind a plot to assassinate former president George H.W. Bush, the current president's father and President Bush wanted revenge. Another theory was that Vice-President Chaney was looking at the oil in Iraq and how the U.S. (mainly Halliburton) could gain control of the oil if we invaded Iraq and used his influence to convince the President to take action. Whether or not any of theories were true, the bottom line is that we invaded Iraq March 2003 and there were no weapons of mass destruction. May of 2003

President Bush declared "mission accomplished". Another quick victory for the U.S. military. Not. It was only the start. Another Vietnam?

WHAT PRICE GLORY?

As a people we generally come together when threatened. Leaders that can declare a victory are popular. Bush was popular and it was re-election time. No one in the Republican Party ran against him. The Democrats ran Senator John Kerry for president. Bush won 31 of the states (286 electoral votes) and over 50% of the popular vote. He was not only popular with the civilians but with the members of the military who felt he would complete the war in Iraq.

I was staying pretty busy hiring veterans to support the war in-country in Iraq and Afghanistan. These were people that would be maintaining military equipment, provide logistics support and training to our Iraqi allies. I was still travelling to the various military bases and attending military job fairs. It was amazing to see the reaction of the American people to our military members. There were many times when I would be at an airport to catch a flight and when troops would come in either to catch a flight or come home for 10 days of R&R and the people would stop and applaud them. Sure was different than Vietnam. The troops deserved the positive attention. They were exceptional individuals. I know, because both of my sons were serving. One was in the Navy as a seaman boarding suspicious ships and then as a corpsman and the other in Army as a tanker crew member in Iraq without a tank. His company being used more like infantry. He was in Falluja and some of the major fights in other areas.

Bush was wrong. The mission wasn't accomplished as he stated in 2003. Basically a civil war had broken out in Iraq. Additionally the jihadist used our presence in Iraq to convenience many in the mid-east to join their cause. We would be sending more and more troops to Iraq and Afghanistan and the fighting was intense.

As I was interviewing personnel leaving the military to return as civilian contractors for our company, it amazed me the number of them that had multiple tours in combat. I'm talking about two, three, or more tours. They were highly motivated patriots who put their country first.

DOMESTIC ISSUES

President Bush may have won the election but by December of 2004 his ratings started to drop even within the Republican Party. The war was costly in many ways but financially it was a disaster. We went to war and unlike other wars didn't do anything to pay for it except borrow more money. The national debt had doubled from what it was in 2000 to $11.3 trillion dollars due to tax cuts and increased security spending. The administration started receiving criticism for abuse of prisoners of war, torture of prisoners with waterboarding, the NSA surveillance program, the Guantanamo Bay Detention Camp, and a real failure in response to Hurricane Katrina in 2005. During the first five years of his administration over 8 million immigrants entered the United States. More any other 5yr period in our history and nearly half were illegal. He wanted a plan that would lead to citizenship for 12 million illegal aliens. That didn't happen. He wanted to privatize social security and that didn't happen. He did make some advancement with the No Child Left Behind Act, Medicare Modernization Act, and Health Savings Account, which helped some for the out of pocket expenses of medical care. When the mid-term election took place in 2006, the Democrats won control of the House and Senate.

By the end of 2007 we were in the longest recession since WWII. As 2008 was coming to an end, oil prices were soaring, we had a mortgage crisis, and unemployment was sky-rocketing.

My opinion: As I mentioned earlier, I had some real reservations about George W. Bush when he first won the nomination in 2000. I think during his first term he was not well served by many members of his administration including his vice-president, but he did grow into the job. He made a lot of questionable decisions but I think during his second administration his heart was in the right place and he started taking control of his administration.

There was a survey question one-time to the public as to who would you enjoy sitting down with and having a beer. The answer was President Bush. He was a nice guy and knew how to laugh at himself.

CHAPTER 13

Barack Obama, Democrat, January 2009 – 2017

The lead-up to and the actual election held in 2008, I found troubling and really got me concerned for the country.

We had some serious problems economically and internationally left over from the final years of George W. Bush's time in office. We had a failure of major financial institutions in process and the wars in Iraq and Afghanistan were still on going. It would take a pretty smart leader to get things under control again.

My party, the GOP, had 5 major candidates running for the nomination for president: John McCain, Mitt Romney, Mike Huckabee, Rudy Giuliani, and Fred Thompson. To me it was a no-brainer, I supported and voted for John McCain to be our candidate. I felt he was the best qualified, an honest man who could work across the aisle with the opposition, a Vietnam vet and war hero who understood the military and sacrifices made, and someone who understood the complexities of the world. I knew he would put the country first.

The Democrats had 6 major candidates: John Edwards, Joe Biden, Christopher Dodd, Bill Richardson, Hillary Clinton, and a young senator named Barack Obama whom I thought was a rising star in the Democratic Party and someday would be a future candidate. I would have guessed at the time they would select either Edwards or Biden. I was wrong. Biden and Edwards didn't make it nor did Dodd or Richardson. It was down to Hillary Clinton and Barack Obama. Obama won.

McCain won the nomination for the GOP. I thought for sure he was going to select Senator Joe Lieberman (a former democrat turned independent) as his running mate, a rather untraditional move, but someone that endorsed him for President and was an experienced senator. Instead he selected Alaska Governor Sarah Palin. Who? That was the question many Americans were asking.

She was the proverbial albatross around McCain's neck. She was a former sportscaster for TV stations in Alaska, mayor of a small town and governor of Alaska prior to her selection as McCain's running mate. It became pretty clear in interviews conducted with her leading up to the

2008 election that she had no idea of international issues and in my opinion at the time would be a terrible president if something happened to John McCain.

The three Presidential debates, were pretty much the norm, McCain talking about international problems and Obama pushing domestic issues, but in surveys conducted afterwards, most people considered Obama the winner. As for the Vice-presidential debates, Sarah Palin didn't do McCain any favors and it showed to me that she had no idea how Washington or the world operated.

In politics it seems that when you are losing at selling your philosophy you turn to false hoods. It was at this time that some of the right-wing conspiracy people and some GOP leaders started the false stories that Obama wasn't a US citizen and was a Muslim. The plan seemed to be to play on people's fears and hatred. I was flabbergasted that the GOP allowed this to go on and on. John McCain was the only GOP politician that I remember that stood up against this nonsense. I saw him on TV at a town hall, and there was a little old lady that said she had fears of Obama because he wasn't a citizen and was a Muslim. McCain took the microphone back from her and made it clear that she was wrong. He spoke up for Obama and reinforced what I believed about McCain, an honorable man who put truth and the country first. I was beginning to wonder about some of my fellow Republicans and their motivations.

THE OUTCOME

As we all know, despite McCain's popularity, Obama won. Obama won about 52% of the popular vote and won with 365 electoral votes to McCain's 173. Why did this happen? For me, I just couldn't handle the idea of Palin as the VP. I know that many of my fellow Republicans felt the same. As for the rest of America, I think America was getting tired of the wars, the economic collapse, and the problems with the powerful people on Wall Street. Obama also reached out to the young people, and the Black voter. He was comparatively younger and a terrific communicator and he understood that we had some serious domestic issues and had answers to them.

His inauguration was mind-boggling. There was approximately 1.8 million supporters in attendance. It was one enthusiastic party. Maybe America was going to grow up and get back on track. I had no objection to some of his ideas and it appeared to me that President Obama didn't object to someone just because they were a Republican. As a matter of fact during his presidency four members of his cabinets were Republican.

He also won my support during his first 100 days in office by suspending the Guantanamo military commissions and ordering the shutdown of the facility within one year and he also banned torture and coercive techniques such as waterboarding. These activities had been hurting us internationally and went against all that I had been taught in the military.

I believe that he was sincere when he stated his believe that there is only one America, not a White, Black, Asian, or Hispanic America. However, many of my friends and acquaintances had other opinions. Mostly it seemed they felt that their world was falling apart. A Blackman had just become president. "Before you know it the Blacks will be taking over the country!" many of them said. I remember one night a young woman approached some of us at the Legion, telling us we needed to get our guns ready because the Blacks were taking over. We told her to leave, but the truth of the matter is that there were many who thought that way. According to the FBI prior to 2008 there were 43 militias in the country. By 2011, they reported 334 militias with 65% of them far right white supremacist groups (hate groups based on race or religion).

I know when President Obama gave his address to congress and was explaining his Affordable Care Act program, I was absolutely shocked when Joe Wilson, Republican Representative from South Carolina called out during the speech that Obama was a liar! A complete lack of respect for the office of President and the decorum of the House. Two weeks later, over $2 million dollars had been donated to Joe Wilson. Not a good sign.

DOMESTIC ISSUES (ECONOMY)

Domestically, Obama enforced the Economic Stabilization Act that the Bush administration and Congress had passed just before he took office. He thought it was unfair to ordinary taxpayers, because it allowed the government to buy hundreds of billions of dollars in bad loans from the banks bailing them out and they were the ones that created the economic crisis but it saved the institutions and the international/national economy. The treasury disbursed $441 billion, buying bank stocks, the bailout of AIG, shoring up the credit markets, and to modify mortgages to keep people in their homes. By the end of 2018, by selling the bank stocks when they were high and banks paying back money loaned, a $4.5 billion profit was made. "Too Big to Fail" was the watch word. It did bother me that the leaders of those institutions were never held accountable for their actions.

February 13, 2009, the administration with support of both houses of congress, controlled by the Democrats, passed the American Recovery and Reinvestment Act. Only three Republican Senators voted for it and no Republicans in the House supported it. The objective was to save jobs, create new jobs, provide temporary relieve to those most affected by the crisis, and invest in infrastructure, education, health, and renewable energy. It was credited with ending the financial crisis in July of 2009. I couldn't understand the lack of support by the GOP other than they just didn't want to do anything they thought might make President Obama look good.

In 2009 the automotive industry was in trouble and on the brink of going bankrupt. This would have affected more than seven million industry related jobs. Not many people supported the idea initially of saving the industry, including President Obama, Mick Romney, and me, but it became clear that not to do so would have been catastrophic. Money was used from the Troubled Asset Relief Program (TARP) saving the industry and guess what. The automotive industry paid the money back and the fund made several million dollars in profit. By the end of 2012, most people, including me, felt it had been a smart move.

Another major step taken because of the crisis was the passage of the Dodd-Frank Wall Street Reform Act and Consumer Protection Act. I am sure that most of us couldn't start to explain what it did, but Kimberly Amadeo, former President of Money Watch and a recognized US Economy Expert in a recent article did a great job of explaining it. It's a law that regulates financial markets and protects consumers. It is designed to prevent a repeat of the 2008 financial crisis. Basically it keeps tabs on the giant insurance companies, bans banks from using or owning hedge funds for their own profit (with your money), reviews Federal Reserve bailouts, monitors risky derivatives, brings hedge fund trades to light, oversees, credit rating agencies, and established the Consumer Protection Bureau which regulates credit cards, loans, and mortgages. It passed in 2010 in the House 223 to 202 (mainly party lines) and in the Senate 59 to 39. Three GOP Senators supported it. The big money people, banks, and insurance companies have been trying to eliminate it ever since it passed. They don't seem to like any regulation or oversight. I thought it was a pretty good law promoting financial responsibility by the firms holding and using my money.

DOMESTIC ISSUES (HEALTH CARE)

One of Obama's primary campaign issues was the healthcare system. We were one of only a few countries in the world that didn't guarantee healthcare to all citizens. If you were poor or low income, odds were you didn't have any health coverage. If you were middle-income you might have health coverage but it was very expensive and took needed funds for things like housing and food away from you. Not all employers provided health coverage for their employees and even those that did still placed a heavy cost-share on the employee. The health insurance companies also could deny you coverage based on preexisting conditions such as heart condition, diabetes, cancer, etc. So what did people do that faced these issues? Either they did nothing maybe leading to early death or worsening of their condition, or they went to the emergency room where they had to be seen and treated by law. Of course they couldn't pay the bill, which meant the hospital had to pass those expenses along to other patients to cover the costs or the taxpayer. The answer was the Affordable Care Act or as the GOP named it "Obamacare".

The argument was that it is "socialism or communism". "The government is going to decide who gets what treatment". "They have death panels that will decide who lives or dies". "It will drive the national debt up" (like borrowing money to fight a war wouldn't). It was all false statements.

I knew people that didn't have medical insurance and they too believed all of the above. Of course once they qualified and got coverage, they thought it was the best thing since peanut butter.

This didn't come about without problems though. The rollout of the program was an administrative disaster. Computer program problems haunted it from the start along with the aforementioned claims. Challenges ended up in court and the GOP spent all their time trying to overturn it, right up until today.

WELCOME TO THE TEA PARTY

The Tea Party was an ultra-conservative group that started demonstrating against Obama Care program and anything else that the administration seemed to try. They compared Obama to Hitler. Even though I disagreed with some of the Democrat programs and actions, I thought that was kind of a stretch. It was promoted as a grass-roots activism movement. It was later reported to actually be financed by some billionaires promoting their own agenda.

With the mid-term elections approaching the GOP expected to make big gains and maybe take back both houses of congress, but many establishment Republicans found themselves at odds with the Tea Party. The Tea Party started backing even more conservative candidates to run against the moderate conservatives of the GOP. They managed to unseat Majority Leader Eric Cantor in his Virginia primary. The Tea Party rented and held a couple of meeting at our Legion Post. Their rhetoric sounding kind of anti-government to me. I didn't think much about it until they held one meeting to talk about firearms and encouraging the purchase of them. Hmm, not what was that all about?

During the mid-term elections the GOP failed to win control of the Senate, but they did take control of the House and many governorships, and state legislatures. John Boehner became Speaker of the House and Mitch McConnell remained Senate Minority Leader. When McConnell was interviewed by the National Journal magazine as to congressional GOP priorities. His reply blew me away, **"the single most important thing we want to achieve is for Obama to be a one term president".** That's it? No new important legislative issues to promote? Why is that the single most important thing? I guess we are giving up on finding common ground on issues and negotiating with the other side.

It struck me right away that McConnell was one of those politicians more interested in personal power than anything else. Maybe that is why Obama wasn't a one term President even though the GOP would take control of the Senate during the 2014 election and try once again to do away with the Affordable Care Act. If not for John McCain's vote it would have happened. I felt that

McConnell was taking the GOP into an obstructionist mode. For example when the vacancy occurred on the Supreme Court, with over a year until the next election, McConnell wouldn't even allow the Senate to consider the President's nominee or anyone until Obama left the White House. The Supreme Court is the third leg of government and shouldn't be politicized. Give the nominee a hearing and if you don't feel the person isn't qualified or won't interpret the law without personal prejudice, vote against the appointment.

As Speaker of the House, John Boehner was another type of person. He had a way of pissing people off and it didn't matter which party you belong to. When the Sandy hurricane relief bill came up for a vote, he adjourned the house instead. Nobody was happy about that. He also got on the wrong side with the "Freedom Caucus" and the Evangelical coalition. Comments were made that he would rather be on the golf course than do the job. Where was Republican leadership?

DOMESTIC ISSUE (IMMIGRATION)

If there is one issue that has plague the country for centuries it has been immigration. No administration has found an answer that pleases everyone and our prejudices definitely cloud how we look at the problem. At one time the Irish, the Italians, the Jews, and other ethnic groups weren't welcome. But by coming here legally and getting their "Green Card" they could eventually become citizens. That's not the problem. It is those that have illegally entered the country.

During the first few years of Obama's administration, it was estimated that there were 11 million undocumented immigrants in the U.S. The President was being criticized by the extremist on both sides of the issue. Deportations were increasing each year peaking at approximately 410,000 in FY 2012. Obama was being called by some as the "deporter-in-chief". The Democrat controlled Senate had a bill for immigration but the Republican controlled House wouldn't consider it.

I think there was a total misunderstanding of Obama's approach to this problem. Here's what the obamawhitehouse.archives.gov said.

"It is just not practical to deport 11 million undocumented immigrants living within our borders. The President's proposal provides undocumented immigrants a legal way to earn

citizenship that will encourage them to come out of the shadows so they can pay their taxes and play by the same rules as everyone else. Immigrants living here illegally must be held responsible for their actions by passing national security and criminal background checks, paying taxes and a penalty, going to the back of the line, and learning English before they can earn their citizenship. There will be no uncertainty about their ability to become US citizens if they meet these eligibility criteria. The proposal will also stop punishing innocent young people brought to the country through no fault of their own by their parents and give them a chance to earn their citizenship more quickly if they serve in the military or pursue higher education".

This seemed like a realistic approach to me, especially for the "Dreamers" those young people who had no say so about coming here and this being the only country they have ever known. The problem was that congress wouldn't do their job and approach the issue.

Obama also wanted to "beef up" security at the southern border and other entry points. He wanted more Border Patrol agents hired, installation of high tech surveillance systems, increased deportation of the criminal elements that are here illegally. But since congress wouldn't act he used an executive order which didn't go over very well with a lot of people. One of the problems with executive orders is that the next President doesn't have to keep it in effect and only congress can pass laws.

This was just an example though how the GOP decided to just not support anything that Obama tried to do. If not for Executive Orders, not much of anything was going to be accomplished. I didn't like it, but that was how it was.

INTERNATIONAL AFFAIRS

Obama opposed the war in Iraq back in 2003. During the campaign for President he promised to withdraw from Iraq as soon as possible. In February 2009 he announced a plan to withdraw over 100,000 troops by August. He projected to have all troops out by end of 2011. Maybe we were finally going to get out of the war and nation building business. Unfortunately it didn't happen.

He also promised to commit to Afghanistan and keep the Taliban from regaining power and letting al Qaeda use the country as a base of power again.

Obama reached out to Israel and the Palestinians for peace accords. He spoke of reducing nuclear weapons throughout the world. He promoted a reset of relations with Russia. Before any of this came to completion he was awarded the Nobel Peace Prize in October 2009. I think he was just as surprised as the rest of us, because nothing had been accomplished yet! However, I believe it lifted him in the eyes of the rest of the world. He didn't sound like a man looking for more trouble to get the country into.

Unfortunately, military conflict doesn't always work out like you think it should. He announced a surge of forces in Afghanistan December 2009 to train the Afghan armed forces rather than fight with the goal of withdraw July of 2011. It seemed to be working and the feather in his cap was the killing of Osama bin Laden May 2, 2011. "Mission Accomplished"? No, his goal to total withdraw wasn't accomplished. He realized that the Taliban were not yet defeated. Here we go again.

His administration decided on a different approach to the terrorist problem and embraced multinational action consisting of air strikes and special operations forces. Libya is a good example. Bombing in support of the rebels kept us out of a ground war, but with the killing of Qaddafi another problem developed, the attack on Benghazi in which our Ambassador was killed along with several others. This also opened up a can of worms at the State Department. The American people were told that the attack was because of an internet video that insulted the Arabs. That wasn't case and led to the Benghazi hearings in congress that lasted more than 2 years and over $7 million dollars of tax payer's money being spent for the hearings.

The President realized that America was tired of being on a "war footing" all the time. In Syria there was a civil war going on. Obama established a red line. If Bashar al-Assad used chemical weapons against the rebels we would respond in their support with air strikes. We didn't strike. Instead the President accepted an offer from Putin to persuade Assad to get rid of his chemical weapons. I believe his international credibility was questioned from that point forward. If you draw a red line, it is supposed to mean something. It also solidified Russia's foothold in the Middle-East.

One positive step in the Mid-East was the beginning of negotiations with Iran to prevent that country from developing nuclear weapons in exchange for removing United Nations sanctions. Iran surrendered 97% of its enriched uranium. There was also a large sum of cash that the US had been holding during the Iranian revolution that was returned to the Iranians. That raised a few eyebrows! The stories began that we bought off the Iranians.

In 2014 the US and China reached an agreement to reduce carbon emissions, another goal towards fighting climate change. A year later at the Climate Change Conference in Paris almost every country in the world agreed to take action and develop plans to save the climate. This would eventually lead to the Paris Climate Agreement that every nation except one agreed to. Maybe we could still save the planet.

International problems in 2014 just wouldn't go away. ISIS, a former al Qaeda group took advantage of the civil war in Syria and took ground between Syria and Iraq to create an Islamic state. The administration's answer was to send 5000 more troops to Iraq and conducted approximately 10,000 air strikes before Obama left office.

If this wasn't bad enough, Putin ordered the attack and occupation of Ukrainian territory. They took and annexed Crimea. Crimea is a major strategic choke-point to the Black Sea. The administration response along with European allies was economic sanctions which brought no results.

THE 2012 ELECTION

President Obama had no challengers from the Democratic Party. The Republican Party had at least 11 people seeking the nomination. Some of the notables included Mitt Romney, Ron Paul, Newt Gingrich, Rick Santorum, Rick Perry, Jon Huntsman Jr., Michelle Bachmann, and Herman Cain. Mitt Romney is who I supported and he had been the biggest fund raiser of the group, but it turned out to be sort of iffy as to who would get the nomination. Five times other candidates took the lead in the polls and primary elections. It was almost as if the party just couldn't get itself together and support anyone. Romney won the nomination and selected Paul Ryan to be his running mate.

Things were looking good for Romney. He even looked better than Obama in the first Presidential Debate, but really messed up several times in the lead up to the election. On an international trip July 2012 he managed to insult several different countries' leaders, discussed the possibility of military strikes against Iran with Israeli leaders, insulted the Palestinians by saying Israel was more successful due to the hand of providence, and even managed to offend Mexico. Later that month he addressed the NAACP and said he will eliminate every non-essential, expensive program including Obama Care. That got him booed by the crowd.

You would think that it couldn't get worse but it did. At a $50K a plate dinner he was recorded talking about taxes and claimed that 47% of the voters supporting Obama didn't pay taxes. They are dependent on the government. **His job wasn't to worry about those people** as there was no way he would ever convince them to take personal responsibility and care for their lives. Well, I guess that's one way to turn off a bunch of voters.

The GOP campaign continued to get worse with false stories being generated that many of the automakers, owned by Italians, which had been saved by the government, were going to build their cars in China. The media had a field day.

President Obama was reelected. He won with 51% of the popular vote. In the Electoral College Obama had 332 votes (less than previous election) and Romney had 206 votes. Instead of the GOP regaining the Senate, they lost seats. With the exception of Florida and Virginia the GOP carried the south and most of middle states.

Following the loss the GOP had a hard look at itself. Reince Priebus was the National Committee Chairman. His response was, "There is no one reason we lost. Our message was weak: our ground game was insufficient; we weren't inclusive; we were behind in both data and digital; and our primary debate process needed improvement". Someone paid attention to the loss! "The party did go on to make progress in the 2014 mid-term elections for House seats becoming the majority and had control of both the Senate and House from 2015 to 2017.

TERRORISM AND NATIONAL DISCOURSE

The Obama years were filled with terrorism, national discourse, and tragedy. We had several domestic terrorist attacks, 25 riots, and according to Wikipedia, at least 70 multiple shootings including school and church shootings, and armed conflicts between civilian groups and the government. The following are some of the better known events:

November 2009, Ft Hood, TX, a radicalized Muslim Army officer shot and killed13 people and wounded 33 others.

August of 2012, an American white supremacist, Wade Page, a member of the neo-Nazi skinhead Hammerskin Nation, and an Army veteran, killed 6 people and wounded four others, in a shooting at the Wisconsin Sikh temple in Oak Creek, WI.

The following year, April 15, 2013 during the Boston Marathon, two homemade bombs exploded killing three and wounding hundreds. Two Kyrgyz-American brothers were behind the attack and claimed they were motivated by radical Islamists beliefs.

July 2015, Chattanooga, TN, a military recruiting center and USNR base was attacked with 5 killed and 2 wounded. FBI said it was motivated by terrorist propaganda.

June 2015, Charleston, SC, a 21yr old white supremacist entered the Emanuel African Methodist Episcopal Church and killed 9 people including a state senator. He had hoped his action would start a race war.

November 2015, Colorado Springs, CO, Planned Parenthood Clinic attack with 3 killed and 9 wounded.

December 2015, San Bernardino, a husband and wife attacked his colleagues at a County Department of Public Health training event and Christmas party. Both had become radicalized through jihadist material on the internet. The attack ended with 14 killed and 22 wounded. Both were killed by police. A search of their home revealed that they had constructed pipe bombs.

June 2016, Orlando, FL, was the Orlando nightclub shooting at the Pulse nightclub (a Gay bar). The killer was a Muslim-American, born in New York of Afghanistan heritage who had been on the FBI watch list for 2yrs prior to the incident. It was reported that 49 were killed and 53 injured.

OTHER MASS SHOOTINGS NOT CONSIDERED TERRORIST

January 2011, Tucson, AZ, 6 killed and 15 wounded, including Representative Gabrielle Gifford giving a speech at a Safeway store.

July 2012, Aurora, CO. At a movie house 12 killed and 70 wounded.

December 2012, Newton, CN, Sandy Hook Elementary school, 20 children and 6 adults killed.

September 2013, Washington Navy Yard Shooting, 12 killed and 8 wounded.

April 2014, Ft Hood, TX, 3 killed, 14 wounded by soldier that had been denied leave.

May 2015, Waco, TX, Motorcycle Club shoot-out, 9 killed, 18 wounded.

October 2015, Colorado Springs, CO a man openly carrying a rifle randomly starts shooting at people, 3 killed and 9 wounded.

November 2015, Minneapolis, MN, during a Black Lives Matter protest 5 people shot and wounded.

(The following may not have been categorized as domestic terrorism but that is debatable)

July 2016, Dallas, TX, following a peaceful protest, escorted by Dallas PD, over two black men who had been shot by police in Baton Rouge, LA and St Paul, MN (Alton Sterling and Philando Castile), officers were attacked by a sniper killing 5 officers and wounding 11, including 2 civilians.

July 2016, Baton Rouge, LA, same as above, with 3 officers killed and 3 wounded. The shooter was identified as a member of a black separatist group and the **Sovereign Citizens** organization.

DOMESTIC ARMED CONFLICT

There were several armed conflicts that stood out to me. In 2014 there was an armed standoff between supporters of a cattle rancher named Cliven Bundy and federal law enforcement over a dispute between Bundy and the Bureau of Land Management (BLM). The dispute had been going on since 1993 when there was a change in the rules regarding grazing of cattle on federal land. Bundy had objected to the rule change and refused to renew his grazing permit or sell it back to the government, and wouldn't remove his cattle despite court orders to do so. He said he didn't recognize the government's authority to regulate grazing rights.

He ended up owing the government $1 million dollars in fees. The court told the BLM to remove the cattle. Bundy resisted and in interviews used the language of the **"Sovereign Citizen"** movement which gained him the support of the Oath Keepers, White Mountain Militia, and the Praetorian Guard. He was at first praised by GOP and conservative talk show personalities but after making some racist comments lost their support.

He left the Republican Party. Three Nevada Tea Party groups gave him their support. Although his cattle had been confiscated, they were eventually returned and he claimed victory of the feds.

This wasn't the last to be heard from the Bundy family. January 2016 armed far-right extremist occupied the Hqtrs for the Malheur National Wildlife Refuge in Oregon for 40 days. They were led by Ammon Bundy, Cliven Bundy's son. They claimed the federal government was required to turn over all federal managed land to the states. By February 11th all the militants had been arrested or had withdrawn from the occupation. One individual, Robert LaVoy Finicum, was shot and killed in an attempt to arrest him. Mr. Finicum had become fairly well known to the public having been interviewed several times on national news networks.

These two events just reinforced my concerns that we could easily end up in a civil war involving militias with radical ideas.

PROTEST AND RIOTS

I have always believed that we have a right to peaceful protest. It is guaranteed in the constitution the right of peaceful assembly.

Unfortunately, quite often the peaceful protest end up in a riot. Normally, after the peaceful people have left. However, sometimes when the authorities show up depending on their actions a riot will break out. This happened in Ferguson, MO, August of 2014.

The protest began over the police shooting of Michael Brown. Brown and his friend had been stopped by a police officer for walking in the middle of the street and noticed Brown had a box of cigars that matched the theft of cigars at a convenience store. An altercation between the officer and Brown resulted in Brown being shot in the hand and then running off. The officer pursued and shot Brown several times in the chest. Brown died at the scene. While waiting for all the backup, investigators and other responders, Brown's body lay in the street. A crowd was angry about this. Witnesses had different stories as to what happened. The Brown family and community wanted charges pressed against the officer. A Grand Jury reviewed the case and declined to indict the officers.

August 12th, the citizens of Ferguson protested in the streets. Law enforcement showed up and told the crowd to disperse. According to the police some bottles were thrown at them and they responded with smoke bombs, flash grenades, rubber bullets, and tear gas. This was all televised. Derogatory language was used by some officers and that night a woman was shot in the head with a rubber bullet. The following night the protest continued with the protestors now throwing projectiles at the police, including Molotov cocktails. Officers responded and began forcefully removing people including members of the press. Reporters from several media were arrested, tear-gassed, and shot with rubber bullets. The police said it didn't happen.

The federal government did an investigation and determined that "Ferguson PD engaged in misconduct against the citizens of Ferguson discriminating against African-Americans, which were the majority of the citizens, applying racial stereotypes in their practice of unlawful conduct. It was also found that Ferguson depended on fines and other charges generated by the police".

This was just one of the events that resulted in rioting during the Obama administration's time in office. I was starting to think that we were falling into the same activities as during the 60's civil rights marches and the anti-war protests during Vietnam.

Naturally the press and politicians took notice of what all was going on but instead of bringing the country together to solve the problems, took advantage for their own gain. What was true just depended on whose side you were on.

MY PERCEPTION OF THE TIME

I really felt that the ugliness of polarization because of race had raised its head again. Based upon how people were talking against Obama and verbally attacked anyone that claimed to be a Democrat that we were heading for trouble. Americans were beginning to openly become tribal in their speech and actions. It looked to me that my political party, the GOP had decided that it was easier to just become obstructionists rather than to find middle ground as we always had in the past. The next election would reveal the truth.

CHAPTER 14

Donald J. Trump, GOP, January 2017 - 2021

I must admit that I was looking forward to the election season. Just who would be stepping up for both sides? What would they be supporting and what would they be against?

It didn't take long to figure out the Democrats. Hillary Clinton, Bernie Sanders, and Martin O'Malley were the only ones running. O'Malley dropped out right away after placing 3rd in Iowa. Clinton and Sanders would go at each other. I thought it strange that Sanders being an Independent was even allowed to get into the Democrat's race and declaring himself a "Socialist Democrat" was crazy. There was no doubt in my mind that they would select Hillary Clinton as their candidate.

My party, the GOP, had 17 people filing for the nomination. Some of the well-known names included Jeb Bush, Chris Christie, Ted Cruz, Carly Fiorina, John Kasich, Marco Rubio, Rick Santorum, Rick Perry, Scott Walker, Ron Paul, Mike Huckabee, and Donald Trump. Donald who? Well this should be an easy win for either Bush or Christie.

TRUMP ANNOUNCES HE IS RUNNING FOR PRESIDENT

The first time Trump ran for a nomination to be President was with the Reform Party in 2000. In his book **The Making of Donald Trump, by David Cay Johnston**, a well-known author and investigator reporter, tells the story of **Trump declaring he would be the first person to run for president and make a profit.** In an interview he said he had a million dollar deal to give 10 speeches at motivational events and he coordinated his campaign events so the campaign would pay for the use of his 727 jet. He dropped out with the start of his reality television show. More money there?

TRUMP ANNOUNCES HE IS RUNNING FOR PRESIDENT (FOR THE 2ND TIME)

I was watching television as he came down the escalator at Trump Tower with his wife. There was a small crowd with signs and cheering him. It turned out that they had been hired to be there. Trump's slogan was "Make America Great Again" and his primary issues were illegal immigration, the national debt, Islamic terrorism, and offshoring of jobs. These were issues that the American public had concerns about but he had some real odd ball ways of addressing them. Trump's remarks about Mexico were mind boggling, **"When Mexico sends its people, they're not sending their best ...They're sending people that have lots of problems, and they're bringing those problems with them. They're bringing drugs. They're bringing crime. They're rapists. And some, I assume are good people."** I sat there stunned. Did he really just say that? Then he talks about how he will build a great wall that will keep the Mexicans out and that Mexico will pay for it! This has got to be a publicity stunt, right?

There was an immediate reaction to Trump's remarks. Many Republicans took offense to what he said and how he said it and so did many leading businesses and organizations who cut ties with him. He stood by his comments but said that his comments were aimed at the Mexican government and not the immigrants themselves. Hmm, there must have been something wrong with my hearing that day.

What a lot of people didn't know was who Trump really was. They accepted the character from his television show as being real. He talked tough, was aggressive in his dealings, and could really carry a grudge against anyone that questioned him. His real success in business generally seemed to be on the marginal side versus how he portrayed himself to the media and the public. Anyone who ever sued him, including the government, generally found themselves in a counter lawsuit. When push came to shove he normally settled quietly with his opposition. Everything I read about him let me to believe he was nothing more than a braggart, and a very questionable, dishonest person, with some serious problems. I was somewhat familiar with Trump's background since he showed up on the cover of the National Enquirer many times over the years and he was a guest on several television shows and on radio. His career was one of constantly searching for publicity. He loved promoting himself and his so called successful business career. With the media coverage he gained with his behavior and statements he made, Trump had more free publicity and exposure than most campaigns could probably afford to buy.

I read several books written by people that knew him. **TrumpNation: The Art of being the Donald, by Timothy O'Brien** was a real eye-opener. O'Brien had revealed what he said was the truth about Trump's wealth, which was extreme exaggeration. Trump tried suing him for $1billion defamation and lost the lawsuit. **The Making of Donald Trump, by David Cay Johnston** went in-depth about Trumps career and his questionable business associates, taxes, and other interesting facts. None of Trump's opponents addressed any of this.

December 2015, Trump's campaign put out a press release calling for a **"complete shutdown of Muslims entering the United States until our country's representatives can figure out what is going on."** Let's see, Mexicans and Muslims, who's next to target?

When the debates began I thought for sure that it would become apparent to the voters that Trump had no idea what he was doing. Boy was I wrong! Trump had no problem attacking and ridiculing his opponents and they let him get away with it. No counter-attack. Nothing was said about the fact that Trump and his businesses had been involved in more than 4000 state and federal legal actions, including 6 bankruptcies. No one mentioned that during the building of Trump Tower he used over 200 Polish undocumented workers or the fact that he was known for "stiffing" contractors and not paying their bills. Apparently the candidates didn't take Trump seriously and failed to do any research on him. By the end of February many of the big names: Jeb Bush, Rand Paul, Mike Huckabee, Chris Christie, Carly Fiorina, and Rick Santorum, and Rick Perry were all gone. They threw in the towel. Maybe that was good. If they couldn't stand up to Trump how would they perform against our adversaries?

Trump with his disregard for political correctness and his unapologetic style of speaking was making ground. He only had three people left to oppose him for the nomination. The strongest was Ted Cruz, who attacked Trump as not being a conservative nor an ethical businessman. Trump in turn attacked Cruz with the most malicious lies.

Trump's friends at the National Enquirer ran a story stating the Cruz's father was involved in President Kennedy's assassination. **He went on to say, "His father was with Lee Harvey Oswald prior to Oswald being, you know, shot. I mean the whole thing is ridiculous. What is this? Right? Prior to his being shot. And nobody even brings it up. I mean, they don't even talk about that – that was reported. And nobody talk about it."**

Trump also challenged that Cruz could even run for President. After all wasn't Cruz born in Canada? Trump said, **"Republicans are going to have to ask themselves the question: Do we want a candidate who could be tied up in court for two years? That'd be a big problem. It'd be a very precarious one for Republicans because he'd be running and the courts may take a long time to make a decision. You don't want to be running and have that kind of thing over your head."**

Trump played to the Evangelicals by also questioning Cruz's faith when he said, **"To the best of my knowledge, not too many evangelicals come out of Cuba, OK? Just remember that, OK? Just remember."**

He also accused Cruz of having extra-marital affairs and attacked Mrs. Cruz's physical appearance compared to his wife. That fired Cruz up and got him mad. Of course all was forgiven once Cruz lost to him.

Trump also lashed out at the media (fake news) even during the primaries and **called the primary elections a rigged system**. Of course later when he did become the presumptive nominee his comments about the GOP primaries changed to,

"You have been hearing me say it's a rigged system, but now I don't say it anymore because I won. It's true. Now I don't care."

Trump also took his anger out on other Republicans who didn't kneel to him for his election. Remember the interview in 2015 where he was asked about John McCain? His remarks were, **"He's not a war hero. He's a war hero because he was captured. I like people who weren't captured."** This from a man that avoided the draft during Vietnam for supposedly have bone splinters, four times!

I also found it interesting during the 5th Primary debate hosted by Hugh Hewitt, that when Hewitt asked Trump which leg of the nuclear triad he believed was most crucial to update, Trumps answers (I call it tap dancing) showed he didn't know what the Triad was. That was a scary thought. When the question was given to Rubio, Rubio explained what the Triad was (Strategic Bombers, ICBMs, and Submarines).

When the time came to vote in the Primary election I supported John Kasich. He appeared to me to be the only one who didn't come across as a candidate only interested in himself and was truthful in his conversations with the voters. As for the rest, it was totally immature, boorish, bullying actions. But Trump won the needed pledged delegates, even though he only had approximately 45% of the Republican voters.

There was talk of challenging Trump during the convention and picking someone else. When he got word of it, he publicly stated that **if that happen there would probably be riots.** Hmm. Was that a veiled threat?

A MESSY GENERAL ELECTION FOR BOTH SIDES

Clinton -

The GOP wanted the presidency really, really, badly. They felt as early as 2014 that Hillary Clinton would probably be the Democrat's candidate, so they started way back then to try and eliminate her. That was the motivation behind the Benghazi hearings. Clinton as Secretary of State was the target of 2yrs of hearings that cost around $7 million dollars. The reason for the hearings became quite clear September 29, 2015 when Kevin McCarthy went on Fox's Hannity show and said, **"Everybody thought Hillary Clinton was unbeatable right? But we put together on Benghazi a special committee, a select committee. What are her**

numbers today? Her numbers are dropping. Why? Because she is un-trustable. But no one would have known any of that had not happened, had we not fought."

Clinton had previously appeared before the committee and on October 22, 2015 appeared a second time. She testified for eight hours, publicly. It was a really weird thing to watch. The hate towards her was quite visible. Representative Jim Jordan (R-OH) accused her of changing her email accounts. The best they got was she admitted making a mistake using private email, but never sent or received anything marked classified. Representative Trey Gowdy (R-SC) who chaired the hearings released the final report July 2016 with nothing showing wrong doing by Clinton.

What we didn't know was that the FBI August 5, 2015 had opened an investigation of Clinton's servers based on an IG request that classified information was on the servers. June of 2016 the Attorney General, Loretta Lynch, met with former President Bill Clinton for 30 minutes at the Phoenix Airport terminal, during the FBI probe. July 2, 2016 the FBI called Clinton in for an interview. July 5th a statement was released that

Director Comey recommends no charges over Clinton emails even though there were over 2100 emails that were or later were classified but had not been marked as classified. Since it is FBI policy not to comment regarding on-going investigations there were questions why the Director of the FBI made the public announcement regarding the investigation and why did the Attorney General meet with Bill Clinton before there was any release. More fodder for the Trump campaign. Then on October 28th, Director Comey notified congress that in a separate investigation, the FBI had newly discovered emails on a computer belonging to a Clinton associate. Finally on November 6th, Comey notified congress there was no change in the FBI's initial conclusions, but the damage was done.

Clinton's problems continued. WikiLeaks released emails indicating that the Democratic National Committee (DNC) had tilted the Primary towards Clinton. Whether it was true or not, I don't know, but it was more ammo for her opposition. If that's not enough, a Clinton PAC in 2016 suspended a Clinton advisor over sexual harassment claims made during her 2008 campaign. Clinton was aware of the allegations at that time but had ignored them.

Clinton didn't help herself any when she publicly called half of the Trump supporters "deplorables" which just fired a bunch of them up and they started carrying signs at rallies identifying themselves as deplorables.

Another mistake she made is she didn't campaign at all in Wisconsin. As a matter of fact she appeared to just ignore states where her campaign figured Trump would win anyway. I guess the voters didn't deserve some of her attention.

Trump –

I figured that Trump was his own worst enemy during the election and there was no way that he would get elected. From his announcement to run for the nomination and attacking Mexicans as rapists and murderers and proposed to build a wall to keep illegal immigrants out of the country, I thought he wouldn't get a single Latino vote. In November 2015 he stated that he supported having a database for Muslims in the U.S. and expanding surveillance of Mosques and then in December 2015 he called for a complete shutdown of Muslims entering the country. He attacked the media as the "enemy of the people" (an old Soviet Union trick), **claimed that the elections were all rigged if he didn't win** (sort of like during the primary), and then at a campaign rally he called upon Russia to find Clinton's missing emails, which is inviting a foreign nation to interfere in our elections. At his rallies he advocated for his supporters to physically attack anyone that protested against him at the rally. Come September 2016, it was revealed that his charity foundation was under investigation for violating New York laws governing charities (supposedly using the money for personal use). The following month it was reported in the New York Times that Trump had declared a $916 million loss in 1995 that would allow him to skip paying federal income taxes for ten years, but the real kicker in October was the release of footage from 2005 where Trump is talking about trying to have sex with a married woman and being able to grope women because of his celebrity status and kissing women without their consent. This was followed by 11 women claiming they were sexually assaulted or harassed by Trump. It was also revealed that Trump as the owner of the Miss USA and Miss Universe Pageants, was known to walk in unannounced to the changing rooms for the young women during the pageant often catching them naked. My first thought was, "there goes the Evangelical vote".

IN A TWEET NOVEMBER 7, 2012, DONALD TRUMP TWEETED "THE ELECTORAL COLLEGE IS DISASTER FOR DEMOCRACY"

When we talk about our democracy and the right to vote, we say one person, one vote and the most popular person wins. That's not true in presidential elections. Based on the constitution each state has so many Electoral College votes and those individuals representing the state actually cast the vote for president and vice-president. However, before this election the winner of the popular vote generally was also the winner of the Electoral College vote, with five exceptions, John Quincy Adams (1824), Rutherford B. Hayes (1876), Benjamin Harrison (1888), and George W. Bush (2000). Many other democracies have copied our constitution almost verbatim with one exception: NO ELECTORAL COLLEGE! **He and I did agree about the Electoral College**.

I don't know about you but for me there were presidential elections where I voted for what I considered the better of two bad choices for President. This time was a little different. I just couldn't bring myself to vote for either major candidate. I supported most of the GOP running, but I ended up voting for someone in Oklahoma that always runs for President just to make a statement. I, like most people, thought for sure that Hillary Clinton would win, but not with my vote. I just knew there was no way that the American people would elect someone like Trump, someone that had never held a political office, a top government post, or served in the military, a very questionable business record, and had some weird ideas about the Presidency. When the results came in Hillary Clinton had 65,853,516 votes (48.5%) and Trump had 62,984,825 votes (46.4%), but Trump won the Electoral College votes (304 to 227). I don't know who was more surprised, me or Trump. He really didn't expect to win. Even his campaign staff was caught off guard. Many of them were already looking for a new job. It was going to be an interesting 4 years. Despite his pledge to "**only hire the best people**", as a Republican, I could only hope that the party and the other two branches of government, could teach Trump how government worked and ensure that our country and form of government would survive and not get carried away with some of the ideas he had stated.

Before Trump was sworn in as the new President other problems jumped up. In mid-November 2016 he agreed to a $25 million dollar settlement against Trump University. He did this to avoid having to testify in a trial on November 28th.

December 24th, he announced that he would dissolve the Donald J. Trump Foundation to avoid conflict of interest appearance, but the NY Attorney General Office said not until they conclude their investigation of the charity.

ONLY THE BEST

When Trump finally got his team together they were mostly some of the "best yes people" he could find with virtually no relevant experience to the position with just a few exceptions. **Trump told the American people that "only he could fix the problems". To be on his team and survive, your first allegiance had to be to him.**

Here's his first team:

Secretary of State – Rex Tillerson, former executive for Exxon Mobile who had business ties with Russia and Putin. Tillerson is said to have not wanted the position but his wife talked him into it. It was reported that he often referred to Trump as a "dumb s.o.b". **Trump would fire him by tweet.**

Secretary of Defense - James Mattis, retired USMC General. One of the best who stood up to the President until he just couldn't tolerate anymore. When he **submitted his resignation with a target date to leave, Trump sent him out two months early.**

Homeland Security – John F. Kelly, retired USMC General. Another great selection but he would be removed from that position and become Trump's Chief of Staff 12/14/18. **He would eventually be fired by Trump**.

CIA – Mike Pompeo, former member of congress. He would eventually become Secretary of State. He was regarded by many as one of the adults in the room, but later came across to me as one of the "yes men" of the administration.

Secretary of the Treasury – Steve Mnuchin, a successful businessman but he would cause a lot of controversy over using government aircraft for personal use. One of the few to make it all the way through four years.

Attorney General – Jeff Sessions, former Senator and the first to endorse Trump for President. He **got caught up in the Special Investigation of Russian interference in the election and had to excuse himself from participating in the investigation.** Made Trump mad. Tried to resign but Trump wouldn't accept the resignation. Later fired by Trump and blasted by Trump on twitter.

US Trade Commissioner – Robert Lighthizer, experienced from former administrations. He survived all four years.

Director of National Intelligence – Dan Coats, former Senator and an excellent pick for the position based on his Senate positions. Regarded as one of the grownups in the room. **Disagreed with Trump on many occasions and was fired by twitter posting 8/15/2019.**

Secretary of Labor – Andrew Puzder, CEO of restaurant chain but had to withdraw from consideration due to lack of confirmation votes.

Health and Human Services – Tom Price, former congressman. **Forced to resign** in May 2017 after 231 days in office. He had spent $1 million dollars of department money for personal travel in private jets and military aircraft and other ethics questions.

Secretary of Energy – Rick Perry, former governor of Texas and presidential candidate. **Resigned from office after arranging an oil deal between Ukraine and some of his supporters**. His name would turn up again in the attempt to overturn the 2020 election.

Secretary of HUD - Ben Carson, former Presidential candidate. No idea how he got the position. No related experience. **Scandal over money spent for furniture in his office as Secretary of HUD.**

Environmental and Protection Agency – Scott Pruitt, former Attorney General for Oklahoma. **One of the most scandal involved members of the Trump team.** Resigned over things like requiring a 24hr security team, excessive travel costs (over $90K in one week), having a secure "phone booth" installed in his office, and receiving free housing, amongst other things. Even when he was Attorney General for Oklahoma there were ethics questions about him. **He had to resign his position at the EPA.**

Secretary of Commerce – Wilbur Ross, businessman, made it all four years, but was **cited for ethics violation, conflict of interest**, ended the 2020 census early, and failed to respond to congressional inquiry.

Secretary of Transportation – Elaine Chao, **wife of Senator Mitch McConnell**. I thought she was a good pick having served as Secretary of Labor under George W. Bush for 8 years. Came from wealthy foreign family with international shipping interest and hundreds of millions of loans with China. **Her ethics were questioned regarding promotion of her father's interest and preferential treatment to projects in Kentucky. The IG for DOT made referral to Justice Department who refused to prosecute. IG fired by Trump**. I have often wondered if Senator McConnell let Trump get away with so much because his wife was part of the cabinet. **She resigned from office** following the attack on the capitol.

US Ambassador to the UN – Nikki Haley, governor of South Carolina. I thought she was a pretty good person but a real politician. **She voluntarily resigned December 2018**. She became a real Trump defender. Still claims him as a friend.

Secretary of the Interior – Ryan Zinke, former congressman. **Resigned from office in 2019 following a series of ethics violations including expensive flight travel.**

Secretary of Education – Betsy DeVos, a **big time political donor** and proponent of charter schools, school vouchers, and school choice. Her family was ranked as the 88th wealthiest in America. Her brother, Erick Prince, was founder of Blackwater. **Resigned following the storming of the capital just 12 days before her term expired.**

Small Business Administration – Linda McMahon, **big political contributor** and entertainment executive for Pro-Wrestling's WWE. **Resigned April 2019** to work Trump's re-election campaign as Chairwoman of a Super Pac that raised $83M.

Office of Management and Budget – Mick Mulvaney, congressman. A fiscal conservative he held the position until October 2019 and then became Chief of Staff to Trump and **started supporting unproven claims by the President and attacking the press.**

Secretary of Agriculture – Sonny Perdue, former governor of Georgia. He was a good choice and remained in the position for the entire presidency.

Secretary Veterans Administration – David Shulkin, a good selection and experienced in the VA. He ended up be **fired by tweet by Trump March 2018.**

Now the reason why I addressed this is because every one of them had to be approved by the Republican controlled Senate. Very few lasted until the end of the administration. A large number of them were forced to resign over ethics and some when they stood up to the President were fired by tweet. Yep, only the best.

OTHER STAFF PLAYERS

The President has the authority to appoint members of his staff without anyone else's approval. Look at how this worked out:

National Security Advisor – Lt General (Ret) Michael Flynn, lasted not even a month. **He resigned over lying to the FBI and was eventually convicted.** Trump kept him from jail by pardoning him.

Chief of Staff – Reince Priebus came on board from the GOP and ended up being **fired** for not always agreeing with the President or his family.

Chief Strategist – Steve Bannon, Brietbart News who was a real promoter of tearing down the government. Forced out of his position by Trump family members. He too would eventually be **found criminal guilty of crimes but pardoned by the President.**

Counselor – Kellyanne Conway, who probably saved the campaign, but whose reputation was ruined trying to protect the President with comments about "alternative facts".

Press Secretary – Sean Spicer, ended up with his GOP career ending by promoting Trump's lies, such as how big was the crowd at the inauguration ceremony. He would be fired.

White House Counsel – Donald McGahn II, who did an excellent job trying to keep the Presidency straight but eventually left over the Trump investigations.

Head Speech Writer/Political Advisor – Stephen Miller a **far-right extremist and anti-immigration proponent** that had worked for Senator Sessions and Steve Bannon. A major player in the future problems for the administration. He survived the four years.

Political Advisor – Ivanka Trump, the President's daughter, with business ties with China that were strengthened after the election.

Political Advisor – Jared Kushner, the President's son-in-law, with business ties in Saudi Arabia and other Middle Eastern countries, and Israel. The Saudis invested $2 billion in his businesses at the end of the Trump administration.

FOUR YEARS OF DRAMA AND DISSENT

2017 – Could the President be a Russian Asset or Just an Autocrat?

Trump gave a pretty dark inauguration speech that lasted about 15 minutes. It was the shortest inauguration speech since Jimmy Carter. He had a reasonable crowd in attendance but nothing near what he claimed as the largest ever. The proof was the pictures that were taken. Never the less it would set the tone of his administration: exaggerations and falsehoods that could be proven wrong. That same day it is reported by CNN that US intelligence briefed Trump on a dossier containing allegations about his campaign and Russia along with unverified claims about his private life. FBI Director James Comey briefed Trump and Trump would take it that Comey was attempting to blackmail him. Of course it was already being hinted at by USA Today, The Washington Post, the New York Times, CNN, and MSNBC that something had been going on between the Trump Campaign and Russia for some time.

January 23rd by executive action, Trump withdrawals from the US Trans-Pacific Partnership that was awaiting congressional approval.

Four days later, the 27th, Trump signed an executive order banning all refugee arrivals for 120 days, and banned travel from seven Muslim majority countries for 90 days. Refugees from Syria are banned indefinitely.

On February 13th National Security Advisor Michael Flynn resigns over lying to the FBI regarding communications with the Russian Ambassador to the US.

On the 28th Trump nominates his first Supreme Court nominee, Neil Gorsuch. No one was happier than Mitch McConnell who had blocked the filling of the position during the Obama administration for a year. I considered Gorsuch a good man but questioned the way it was done. Neil Gorsuch was confirmed for the Supreme

Court a major win for the Trump administration and Senate Leader Mitch McConnell. The vote was primarily among party lines. McConnell used the "nuclear option" eliminating the filibuster rule which allowed a simple majority to approve a justice to the Supreme Court.

On May 3rd, FBI Director James Comey confirms during a congressional hearing that there is an investigation regarding the Trump campaign and Russia. Less than a week later Comey finds out while visiting the FBI in California, during a news broadcast, that he has been fired. This was the start of the trend of how Trump would fire people that disagreed with him or he considered to be a RINO, Republican in Name Only. Shortly after the firing the FBI opened an investigation as to whether Trump had been working on behalf of Russia against American interest. Former FBI Director Robert Mueller was appointed as special counsel to lead the probe into Russian meddling in the election and potential collusion between Trump campaign associates and Russian officials. Deputy Attorney General Rod Rosenstein had to make the appointment since AG Jeff Sessions had recused himself in March from the investigation. Trump was pretty upset with Sessions for his recusal and it would eventually lead to his firing. I made a comment to my wife and some friends that I wouldn't be surprised if Trump was impeached before long and removed from office.

Later in the month while on his first overseas trip as President, Trump went first to Saudi Arabia. This raised some eyebrows and would later lead to some speculation that it was more for helping his son-in-law with future financial gains than anything else.

On the trip during either at the NATO summit in Brussels or the G7 summit in Sicily he is seen physically pushing aside one of the foreign leaders so that he would be at the front of the picture being taken. It was embarrassing to watch.

In June Trump announced that the US was withdrawing from the Paris climate accords, making us the first nation to do so of the 175 countries that had signed the agreement. June is also the month that the members of congress gather for their annual baseball game. On the 14th as the Republican members gathered for practice a gunman, James Hodgkins opened fire on them wounding 6 people. He was angry over the election of Trump and seeking revenge. The division in the country had turned violent. Where would it end?

President Trump met with Putin in person for the first time at the G20 meeting. What should have been a short meet and greet turned into a 2 hour discussion the subject matter unknown as Trump made the interpreter destroy the record.

Once again the Republican controlled Senate failed to repeal the Affordable Care Act and replace it with their own version, thanks to Senator John McCain voting NO.

In August North Korea made some nuclear threats to which Trump warned that "North Korea will face fire and fury like the world has never seen." North Korea responded that they were examining operational plans to strike the areas around Guam. This was the start of the "Big talk" concerning use of military action by tweet.

Mid-August there was a movement to take down statues of Confederate generals in Charlottesville, Virginia. In response, neo-Nazis showed up in mass for a "Unite the Right rally, resulting in violence, leaving one dead and 19 others injured when a rally protester drove his car into a crowd of counter protesters. Two law enforcement officers were also killed when their helicopter crashed while monitoring the protests. The news media broadcasted the neo-Nazis marching with torches shouting "the Jews will not replace us!" Very reminiscent of the Nazis in Germany during Hitler's reign of terror. During an impromptu press conference at Trump Tower, **Trump declared that there were "fine people" on both sides.** His statement led to an uproar against him. Many people felt that he was more with the racists and extreme right, than the average American. This was further enhanced when he unilaterally, without consulting Justice Department lawyers, pardoned Arizona Sheriff Joe Arpaio who was convicted of criminal contempt in a racial-profiling case.

At the beginning of September the administration announced that it was ending the DACA program which protected 800,000 undocumented immigrants that were brought to the US as children. This program was a result of an executive order during the Obama administration. Trump told Congress they should introduce legislation for the program. The Federal Courts and judges delayed ending the program. Towards the end of the month a third version of the travel ban was unveiled. It restricted travel from Iran, Libya, North Korea, Somalia, Syria, Venezuela, and Yemen, but was blocked by a federal judge in Hawaii and Maryland. But the Supreme Court ruled in December 2017 that the travel ban could take effect pending appeals.

As if there weren't enough controversial problems politically, nature raised her ugly head to challenge Trump. Besides a large number of tornados and fires throughout the country which the federal agencies had trouble responding to due to a failure to appoint people to the leadership roles, hurricane season started.

September 6th, Hurricane Irma, a category 5, touched Puerto Rico causing excessive damage, followed on September 20th, by Hurricane Maria. The island was devastated. No water, no power, thousands left homeless with no resources available to help.

Isobel Thompson wrote in Vanity Fair, May 30, 2018 a devastating report of Trump's response to Puerto Rico. She reports that the New England Journal of Medicine estimated 4,645 residents died in Puerto Rico, 70 times higher than the official toll of 64. **She writes, about Trump saying, "Texas & Florida are doing great but**

Puerto Rico, which was already suffering from broken infrastructure & massive debt, is in deep trouble," he tweeted, "It's (sic) old electrical grid, which was in terrible shape, was devastated. Much of the Island was destroyed, with billions of dollars owed to Wall Street and the banks, which, sadly, must be dealt with. Food, water and medical are top priorities – and doing well."

I remember watching the news when Trump finally arrived in Puerto Rico two weeks after the storm. He made the mandatory tour of damage, had his picture serving food, tossed paper towels at a press gathering to survivors like he was at a party, and met with the Puerto Rican Governor and Mayor of San Juan. His comparison of the lives lost to Maria compared to Hurricane Katrina was shocking, calling Katrina "a real disaster". He asked the governor what the death count was, "16 compared to literally thousands?" Wrong!

In comparing what happen to Puerto Rico versus Texas it is interesting how the government responded to aiding the two. The difference in support to Texas, a Republican state, and Puerto Rico, a Democrat voting area told a story of how Trump regarded American citizens. He even explored the possibility of maybe being able to

sell Puerto Rico to another country. Hmm. Maybe Russia or China would buy it. It would make a great location for missiles.

The fourth quarter of the year wasn't getting any better for the administration. The investigations by the FBI, Mueller, and the Senate started producing some public results. Paul Manafort and Rick Gates surrendered to the FBI on charges of conspiracy and money laundering between 2006 and 2015. Trump goes on twitter and states those actions were from years ago, "there is NO Collusion". Then George Papadopoulos, who was a foreign policy advisor to the campaign, pleads guilty to lying to the FBI about meeting with Russians in 2016. Trump responded by describing him as a "young, low level volunteer, and a liar".

Attorney General Sessions testifies to the House Judiciary Committee that **he now recalls learning of contacts between Russia and the Trump campaign,** but refuses to state whether or not Trump asked him to hinder the Russian investigation. It also comes out from the Senate investigation that Jared Kushner failed to submit to them numerous documents concerning WikiLeaks and a "Russian backdoor overture" which would allow contact during the campaign without the US government knowing it.

President Trump made a 5 nation tour of Asia. During a press conference with the Prime Minister of Japan, Trump encouraged Japan to shoot down North Korean missiles. Now there's a great way to start a war. While this is going on there is a German news release, the Paradise Papers, stating that the Secretary of Commerce, Wilbur Ross, holds a large stake in a shipping company which has ties to Putin's family. Ross denies it, then later says he will "probably" sell his stake in the company. I don't believe he ever did.

Trump did travel to China and meet with President Xi Jinping. He signed a number of binding and non-binding gas, aviation, communications, and food crop deals with China. **Referring to the trade imbalance, he praised China for "taking advantage" of previous administrations!**

We all got a Christmas present in December. Former National Security Advisor, Michael Flynn pleaded guilty to lying to the FBI on January 24, 2017, concerning contacts with Russian Ambassador Sergey Kislyak. Trump's lawyer John Dowd said that Trump knew that Flynn had likely lied to the FBI. When Trump was asked if he would pardon Flynn he replied, "We'll see what happens".

You know the old saying "where there is smoke, there is fire"? There was an awful lot of smoke during the first year of the administration. All I could do was hope the country didn't burn down.

WERE THERE ANY SUCCESSES OR GOOD NEWS FOR THE PUBLIC?

The tax-cut bill which slashed corporate tax rate from 35% to 21% and reduced individual rates. Sounds good? It increased the deficit over $1 trillion. The 400 wealthiest Americans (billionaires) paid a lower rate than the bottom 50% of the taxpayers. **The reduction of the rate for individuals expires in 2025 while the corporation rate has no expiration**. With the elimination of many deductions that individuals could take, it did simplify filing my taxes.

Neil Gorsuch's nomination to the Supreme Court. This more a victory for Mitch McConnell who blocked Obama from filling the seat vacated when Justice Scalia died. Trump did nominate and the Senate approved 12 appellant court judges.

Roll-back of regulations. This was a Trump promise when he ran for election and by executive order made it happen.

The travel ban. Trump told his supporters that he would be tough on immigration and he was by banning most travelers from Muslim nations and stepped up raids on immigrants illegally in the country. He didn't make any progress on his promise to build a wall. Apparently Mexico didn't want to pay for it.

Withdrew from the Paris climate deal. Another campaign promise kept but I don't think it was a smart move. Climate change is real.

Pulling out of the Trans-Pacific Partnership. Campaign promise kept. I think though that it hurt the US and strengthened China.

2018 – Seeds of Autocracy, Threats and Taking Revenge

This year was the year of "Temper Tantrums". Trump was striking out at anyone that disagreed with him or questioned him, and made all kinds of accusations against the press, members of government, and our foreign allies. He was even turning on the people that helped him get into office. Very few members of the Republican Party would speak up against him. Those that did were attacked and identified as RINOs. This became the story that we would see during his entire time in office. His actions were starting to turn-off a lot of people that had voted for him and this was the year for mid-term elections.

He attack the DOJ on twitter as the "deep state", issued a statement that Steve Bannon, his former CEO on the campaign, as having little to do with his win, and after Bannon described to Michael Wolf, in his book Fire and Fury, the meeting between Trump Jr., Manafort, and Kushner and the Russians, and called it treasonous and unpatriotic. Trump said Bannon had lost his mind. He called the book "a phony full of lies, misrepresentations, and sources that don't exist." In answer to charges against him in the press he said he was going to review the "libel laws" saying that they were a sham.

It comes out in the news and verified by Senator Durbin, that in a meeting with Senators Lindsey Graham and Dick Durbin on immigration, that he referred to Haiti and African countries as "shithole countries" and expressed preference for immigrants from Norway, a predominately all white country.

The firing and resignations of people in the State Department and other government agencies started building up including ambassadors, senior career diplomats and DOJ. It was a complete teardown of the institutional government. Trump took a special dislike to Deputy FBI Director, Andrew McCabe, who resigned his post but remained with the FBI pending his soon to be retirement. Two days before his retirement date he was fired which deprived him of his retirement.

Following his State of the Union address, where Democrats didn't applaud him, Trump said that the Democrats were un-American and treasonous for not applauding.

Before the end of the first quarter, White House Communications Director, Hope Hicks resigned, National Security Advisor H.R. McMasters (retired general officer) resigns, his chief economic advisor resigns, and then Trump fires the Secretary of State, Rex Tillerson, and fires the Secretary of Veterans Affairs, David Shulkin.

In a speech to GOP donors at Mar-a-Lago, Trump says, **"it is great" that Chinese President Xi Jinping was able to become "president for life" and that "maybe we will have to give that a shot**

someday". Do you think he was just trying to be funny? I didn't.

The second quarter wasn't much better for the administration. The FBI raided Trump's lawyer Michael Cohen's home which will lead to bigger problems in the year. Homeland Security Advisor Thomas Bossert, National Security spokesperson, Michael Anton, and the Deputy National Security, Nadia Schadlon resigns.

At the G7 summit Trump gets angry about the fact that at a cocktail party some of the other leaders are seen mocking him including the Canadian PM. Angry, he withdraws the US endorsement of the G7 communiques and then calls Canadian PM Justin Trudeau "Very dishonest and meek".

The second half of the year was a continuation of the nutty stuff going on. In the news we saw the terrible conditions that the children being brought across the border were living in and how they were being separated from their parents. This riled up many Americans and drove the divisions wider.

Scandals continued with Trump appointees like Scott Pruitt and Ryan Zink being forced out over their conduct. In an interview with CBS Trump says the European Union is a foe of the U.S. During a summit with Putin, Trump refuses to acknowledge Russian interference with the 2016 election and says it is all a big hoax, despite what his intelligence people tell him. In anger for former top level officials' criticism he publicly considers revoking the security clearances of John Brennan, James Clapper, James Comey, Susan Rice, Andrew McCabe, and Michael Hayden. All well respected people from previous administrations. He finally tweets that AG Sessions should "stop this rigged witch hunt now". The following day Sarah Huckabee Sanders, WH Press Secretary, calls the new media, "the enemy of the people", a terrible choice of words since that was what the Soviets and the Nazis called a free press.

Trump's ego got a little insulted when he addressed the United Nations General Assembly. He said, "The Trump administration has accomplished more than almost any administration in the history of the U.S., so true." The representatives laughed, to which he immediately said to them, "I had not expected that kind of reaction". He also described himself as a "Nationalist".

By fall several other key people were voluntarily resigning or asked to resign. UN Ambassador Nikki Haley and WH Chief Counsel Donald McGahn resign. AG Sessions resigns at Trump's request, General (ret) John Kelly resigns as WH Chief of Staff and is replaced by Mike Mulvaney, and General (ret) James Mattis resigned as Secretary of Defense and gave notice of when he would depart rebuking Trump's foreign policy. Trump kicked him out early. So much for "his" Generals. They were now all gone and he had nothing good to say about any of them, except for Lt General (ret) Michael Flynn, from that point on.

It's not unusual during mid-term elections in the House, for a change of the political party making up the majority. The Democrats won the majority in the House of Representatives by a substantial margin and won many of the state elections. I wasn't too surprised. Many of my fellow Republicans were upset with what was going on with Trump's rhetoric and actions as were many other Americans with the no accountability being exercised by congress for his actions. Unfortunately there were many of the extreme left elected. The divisions within the country worsened. The GOP did retain control of the

Senate. I was rather surprised that the GOP leadership didn't make any attempt to reign the President in some. The writing was on the wall, your loyalty was to him first.

With the murder of Washington Post reporter Jamal Khashoggi at the Saudi Embassy in Turkey, Trump defended the Saudi government saying that it was "rogue killers" responsible. When the CIA told him that the Saudi Crown Prince was responsible, Trump rebuffed the agency. Once again he wouldn't listen to his intelligence agencies.

Trump's former lawyer, Michael Cohen, pleaded guilty to lying to Congress in relation to the Mueller investigation regarding the accusation of working a deal during the 2016 election with the Russians to build a Trump Tower in Moscow. Previously Trump had stated that there was no deal being made, but then said there was nothing wrong with the unsuccessful personal business deal with Russia during the election. So which is it, a deal being discussed or not? Trump turned on his lawyer and wanted harsh sentence for Cohen, but then turns around and praises Roger Stone for not cooperating with the Mueller investigation.

Not much was coming out about where the Mueller investigation was going. The former Attorney General was keeping a tight lid on everything, but he did something that really bothered me. Mueller filed court documents recommending no jail time for Michael Flynn based on Flynn's cooperation during the investigation.

Details soon emerged of attempts by Trump to get the DOJ to prosecute his political enemies, i.e. Hillary Clinton and James Comey. Interestingly enough when it came out that his daughter, Ivanka, was using her personal email for official business, Trump defended her. Isn't that what got Hillary in trouble and was one of his campaign points?

Trump was having problems with his immigration policy. The U.S. Appeals Court ruled against him. Trump called the court ruling "a lawless disgrace" and threatens retaliation. Chief Justice Roberts responds defending the impartiality of the court. Trump responds with a tweet against Roberts. In another controversy move, Trump authorizes troops at the U.S./Mexico border to use lethal force and he threatens to close the entire Southern Border. Not much progress was being made on his "wall" which was actually a fence. Most of the money and construction accomplished was more of repair to existing fencing than building new wall. He finished up the year shutting down the Federal government, over no funding for the wall, from December 22nd to December 31st.

What would 2019 bring?

2019 – The War for Democracy Starts

With the Democrats now in control of the House it was pretty obvious to me that things were about to heat up between them and the Trump administration. During the first meeting of Trump and the Democrat leaders in January, Trump just abruptly walked out of the meeting. There was just no way that he going to recognize that Congress was an equal branch of the government. Neither side was going to respect the other. During the State of the Union address, Nancy Pelosi tore up her copy of his speech at the conclusion which made a public statement of her feelings about Trump.

In February Bill Barr was confirmed as Attorney General. Barr had previously held the position under a former administration. I thought at the time that perhaps some normality would return with his appointment. The following month Mueller completed his report of the investigation of the 2018 election and whether or not there had been Russian interference or other irregularities and submitted it to Barr. The AG two days later released a four page summary to congress and said that Trump hadn't colluded with Russia and the opinion that whether obstruction was committed was found to be inconclusive. Mueller disputed the AG's claim, as was eventually made public. I read the report once it was available, all 448 pages, at least three times. The investigation had produced 37 indictments with 7 guilty pleas or convictions and illustrated that Trump had obstructed justice on multiple occasions and that Trump had refused to answer questions about his efforts to impede the investigation and influence the testimony of witnesses. The report stated that if the Special Counsel's Office felt they could clear the President of wrong doing they would have said so. Instead the report explicitly states that it "does not exonerate" the President and explains that the Office of Special Counsel "accepted" the DOJ policy that a sitting President can't be indicted. Say what?

Mueller was referring to a memorandum written in 1973 by the DOJ Office of Legal Counsel, Robert Bork. It was his opinion that the indictment or criminal prosecution of a sitting President would unconstitutionally undermine the capacity of the executive branch to perform its constitutionally assigned function. This is just a memorandum. **Article II, Section 4 of the constitution doesn't support this memorandum. It refers to removal from office (impeachment) and refers to "if convicted" of high crimes and misdemeanors. Conviction comes from criminal proceedings in a court of law. The DOJ memo means, a President could commit any crime including murder and not be held criminally responsible.** Does that make sense? Mueller took what I consider to be the easy way out, maybe congress would impeach. Nope, the whole matter just seemed to fade away except on several of the more liberal "news" programs.

The House Judiciary Committee did stay active during the month of May trying to get some of their questions answered about the Muller report. AG Barr had appeared before the Senate Judiciary Committee, but basically blew off the House. They had demanded a copy of the unredacted version of the Mueller Report which he failed to deliver and ended up holding him in Contempt of Congress. The House also tried to get Trump's tax returns going so far as to issue a subpoena to the Treasury and IRS. The Trump administration rejected the subpoena. The DC District Court rejected Trump's bid to quash the House Oversight Committee's subpoena for the tax records from his accounting firm. In addition the DOJ blocked former White House Counsel, Don McGahn from testifying to Congress about the Mueller Report. Why?

Mueller formally resigned as Special Counsel on May 29th and spoke about his report. Nothing really new was said. He looked like a whipped puppy dog to me. He did end up on July 24th testifying before the House Judiciary and Intelligence Committees. According to CNN, he deferred or declined to answer questions from members of Congress 82 times. Of those instances Mueller referred lawmakers to his report at least 4 times. It appeared to me that he was pretty frustrated that apparently quite a few of them hadn't read the report. He was hinting that the House had the power to do something about it but no move for possible impeachment occurred.

The administration was still on the warpath about building a wall between the US and Mexico. Trump actually declared a National Emergency to get the funding for the wall. That same day he signed a border security measure negotiated by Congress with almost $1.5 billion set aside for barriers. Trump also threatened to institute tariffs against Mexico. He eventually drops the threat once a deal is made with Mexico over Latin American immigration. It was also announced that he had appointed Stephen Miller, who was a speech writer, to be in charge of the administration's immigration policy. I felt that was a terrible decision placing someone with no experience into such a position especially with his reputation of being prejudice regarding all minorities and immigrants. Then again his thinking was in line with Trump's. Trump would later tell Representatives Alexandria Ocasio-Cortez, Rashida Tlaib, Illhan Omar, and Ayanna Pressley to "go back" to their home countries. I didn't agree with their politics but with the exception of Omar who was a naturalized citizen, the others were natural-born US citizens elected by their constituents. I guess their names didn't sound American enough for him.

Obviously 2019 was going to continue to be on a questionable course. China has been a competitor of ours for years. Most of our electrical components such as computer chips for our cars, computers, cell phones and almost anything else electrical, many of our clothes, and other consumables come from China. To show how tough he could be in negotiations, Trump placed tariffs on over $200 billion dollars' worth of Chinese imports. That didn't hurt China but it did the American consumer. The costs of a tariff is passed on to the consumer not the manufacturer. I couldn't believe how many of my friends and fellow Republicans thought that was being tough on China!

It was no surprise to anyone that Trump would run for reelection. In May the New York Times reported that Rudy Giuliani, Trump's personal attorney was investigating former Vice President Joe Biden regarding his son Hunter Biden's relationship with a Ukrainian energy firm. Why? Biden would be a potential opponent in the 2020 election. Here we go again. In an interview with ABC News Trump said he would be willing to accept information from a foreign government about a political rival and wouldn't necessarily call the FBI about it. **That is not legal folks!** Didn't he remember the last election? June 18th, he held a rally in Orlando, Florida to announce the formal launch of his campaign. That same month he became the first President to step foot into North Korea. According to Trump he and the North Korean Leader had become best friends. He even stated that they had a "love affair".

Since Trump faced no repercussions from the Mueller Report he apparently felt he could get away with anything. With the election coming up in 2020 and former Vice President Biden being a likely candidate, Trump wanted to insure that Rudy Giuliani's attempts in Ukraine to get dirt on Biden would work. In a phone conversation with the Ukrainian newly elected President who needed help with security aid ($400 million) that Trump had blocked, Trump asked for a "favor". He wanted the Ukrainians to get involved in the election by opening an investigation of Biden. Basically, he was blackmailing them with the promised aid. Help him or no money. The conversation had been "classified" and put on a special server so no one would know about it. Fortunately, a whistleblower filed a complaint about Trump's conduct on the call. Despite all attempts to cover up the call the House Intelligence Committee succeeded in getting the acting Director of National Intelligence to share the whistleblowers complaint. The next day the Trump administration lifted the hold on military aid for Ukraine. This led to the Speaker of the House opening an impeachment inquiry. Despite this, Trump says that both Ukraine and China should investigate corruption involving Biden and his family.

The public impeachment hearing began in mid-November and were televised. The witnesses were very convincing. The vote to impeach would take place in mid-December. I thought for sure that even Republican members of congress could see what was going on and would respond just like they did with Nixon. To my amazement they didn't. Even though on the floor of the House the vote was to impeach charging the president with high crimes and misdemeanors (abuse of power and obstruction of congress), the vote was primarily along party lines. No Republican support and three Democrats voted against. It would now go to the Senate for trial.

While all this was going on there had been a change in US policy regarding the war in Syria. In

October during a phone call with the Turkish President, Trump announced that we were pulling our troops out of Northern Syria so that the Turk's could military attack the Kurdish forces which had been our allies against ISIS. **One autocrat looking out for another**?

2020 – Death in America, the Teflon President, and the election

In January Trump was able to take a few victory laps. He had ordered an airstrike against Qsaem Soleimani the leader of the Islamic Revolutionary Guards Quds Force. Soleimani had been behind many of the attacks against US forces in the Middle East and supposedly was planning another attack. This guy deserved to die. However, in response Iran launched a multiple missile attack against two of our Iraqi bases. Even though no deaths were reported and despite his downplaying the Iranian attack, 109 US service members suffered traumatic brain injuries. He tried to pass it off as no injuries just headaches but the truth came out. There was no retaliation for the missile attack. Probably for the best as we otherwise would have been at war with Iran.

He could also brag on the signing of the US-Mexico-Canada agreement into law, replacing the

North American Free Trade Agreement which many claimed was just a name change. In keeping with his targeting of Muslims, he expanded the travel ban to include six additional Muslim countries.

Covid-19

While all political stuff was going on a new danger was facing America. CDC Director Robert Redfield was notified by his counterpart in China of a mysterious illness developing. Redfield notified Health and Human Services Secretary Alex Azar who shares the info with the National Security Council who in turn includes the information in the President's Daily brief. HHS convenes a task force to figure out what is going on. When Azar briefs the President about the disease, Trump calls him an "alarmist". Before the end of January we had our first case in the US. When asked about it by a reporter, Trump said he "was not concerned, it's totally under control". He even praised China for their efforts to control their outbreak. Trump had received a private memo from Peter Navarro, one of his economic advisors, in January and again in February that coronavirus could become a pandemic that could infect hundreds of millions of Americans, and result in the deaths of 1-2 million

Americans and cause trillions of dollars in economic damage. Unfortunately while Navarro was telling this to the President privately, publicly he stated that the American people had nothing to worry about with the coronavirus.

Trump wasn't honest with the public from the start about the outbreak. Despite advice and warnings from the CDC and other advisors, he wouldn't tell the public the truth. By March 9th, cases were increasing in multiple states yet Trump made a public statement that "the virus is very much under control" and less deadly than the flu. Nine days later in a personal interview with Bob Woodward he said, "I always wanted to play it down. I still like playing it down, because I don't want to create a panic". Then in an oval office address he told the American public that "The vast majority of Americans, the risk is very, very low". By the end of March, over 3100 Americans had died and we had over 164,000 cases. By the end of the year over 300,000 had died (that's one out of every 1000 Americans) and we had 19 million confirmed cases of Covid.

Before the outbreak of Covid-19 in the US, we had a strong economy with low employment, but in March 2020 we got hit hard. We had no defense.

In response and in attempt to slowdown the spread of the virus businesses, major league sports, and restaurants began shutdowns. Local governments enacted measures to try to slow the spread. Unemployed became a major problem so bad that by the end of April there were over 20.5 million jobs lost.

I have to give Trump credit for trying to take supportive actions. Emergency action was needed. When he signed the Coronavirus Preparedness and Response Supplemental Appropriations Act, approximately $2.5 billion in aid was provided to local governments and for research for a vaccine. This was followed by the CARES Act which gave every adult a one-time payment of $1200, plus $500 for every child. Small business was granted billions in grants and loans. Trump signed another $484 billion in aid by the end of April. By the end of summer, Trump signed an executive order that created the Lost Wages Assistance Program, extended the moratorium on student loan programs, and Congress agreed to another stimulus package of $900 billion. That gave another $600 direct check to Americans, extended unemployment and the eviction moratorium. These were all excellent and positive actions that he could have highlighted and been proud of. Thanks to his "Operation Warp Speed" we had a vaccine available by December 2020, unheard of development results in such a short time.

Trump wasn't responsible for the virus but he was responsible for the irrational way the people reacted to it. During the many daily briefings given to the public on the virus he would come up with some of the craziest things to say. In an April briefing he said to Deborah Birx, his WH Coronavirus Response Coordinator during the televised briefing, "So supposing we hit the body with a tremendous , whether it's ultraviolet or just very powerful light, and I think you said that hasn't been checked, but you are going to test it. And then I said supposing you bring the light inside the body, which you can do either through the skin or in some other way. And I think you said you're going to test that too. Sounds interesting, right? And then I see the disinfectant, where it knocks it out in a minute, one minute. And is there a way we can do something like that by injection inside or almost cleaning, because you see it gets in the lungs and it does a tremendous number on the lungs. So it'd be interesting to check that." The look on her face was one of shock and disbelieve. What did he just say?

Guess what, people took his word on the disinfectant idea and tried it. Some got terribly sick and some died. Some people even tried other crazy things that either he would promote or a member of his political or media team that resulted in death or terrible consequences for them.

Trump would come up with many different nonsensical statements during the year like, the virus will disappear with the heat, the virus will disappear one day like a miracle, if we stop testing so much the numbers won't be so high, the virus is a hoax, and then he started calling it the China Virus, it was their fault not his. His China Virus title took on a dangerous tone. The next think you know, Asian Americans were being attacked on the streets. They were being held responsible for the virus by radical groups and individuals. He never said a word in their defense. Why would he do these things? It was an election year and he didn't want any of the blame. Trump was always a defensive person that never accepted responsibility when things went wrong and it really showed during the pandemic.

The really sad thing is that he wouldn't be straight with the people like a real leader would be. Even when he pushed to get a vaccine developed and did an outstanding job of making it happen, he failed to emphasis the accomplishments of the research and development. He was an opponent to wearing masks as recommended and held many events that ended up being hotspots for the spread of the virus. Eventually, he would come down with Covid. Fortunately for him he had access to treatments that weren't available at the time to the general public and he recovered.

The Teflon President

Let me introduce you to a man named John Gotti. Some of you may recognize the name, many of you won't because you are too young. John Gotti in 1985 took over the Gambino crime family in New York City. He was responsible for the murder of Paul Castellano, the head of the crime family and Gotti's boss. Gotti became one of the most powerful and dangerous crime bosses in the US. He was quite a character. Unlike most in the mafia, he loved the press and they loved him. **He was quite outspoken with a very entertaining personality as demonstrated on the nightly news.** He was also known for his very dapper way of dressing up. Nothing cheap about his style. **The public loved the guy and his style.** He was given the name of "The Dapper Don" by the media. That name would change in the late 1980 time frame.

Gotti was the target of the FBI and local law enforcement. **Three times he went to high profile trials. Three times they failed to convict him. After that the media referred to him as "The Teflon Don" because the government couldn't make anything stick.** Later it was revealed that the reason for their failure was that the juries had been tainted by jury tampering, juror misconduct, and witness intimidation. He loved the attention and started believing that he really was untouchable. It wasn't until 1991 that they were able to nail him for his crimes and that was only because his underboss, "Sammy the Bull" turned state's evidence against him. He was convicted of 5 murders, conspiracy to commit murder, racketeering, obstruction of justice, tax evasion, illegal gambling, extortion, and loansharking. He received life in prison without parole. Gotti died in prison in 2002.

Why do I bring this up? Trump reminded me of John Gotti. They have the same brash style, feel superior to everyone else, a real know it all attitude, demanded absolute loyalty to them of people, revengeful, and don't accept that the rules apply themselves. I thought though that after the house impeachment maybe Trump would get the wakeup call of his life. He didn't.

When the impeachment went to the Senate for trial the Republican Party had the majority. It takes a 2/3 majority to convict a President and remove him from office. I had observed over the last couple of years that the GOP had started falling in line with Trump but had hoped they would live up to their oaths to the Constitution. In January the Republican controlled Senate voted to reject the Democrats request of 11 amendments to have subpoena authority to introduce testimony from current and former White House officials and rejected subpoena authority for White House documents which were not provided to House investigators.

Senator Mitch McConnell was advising GOP Senators to craft their responses to their own political needs. He even admitted that he was coordinating with the White House and would follow their lead on the trial. Lindsey Graham who was the Chairman of the Senate Judiciary Committee said, "I am trying to give a pretty clear signal that I have made up my mind. I am not pretending to be a fair juror here … I will do everything I can to make (the impeachment) die quickly. McConnell would state, "I'm not an impartial juror. This is a political process. There is not anything judicial about it. Impeachment is a political decision."

So much for the Constitution which mandates that senators must take an impeachment oath in which Senate rules states, "I will do impartial justice according to the Constitution and laws, so help me God". Talk about a tainted jury. Eat your heart out Gotti.

I felt that the House Impeachment Committee did an excellent presentation despite the Senate not allowing and witnesses or White House documents, but the writing was on the wall before they ever got started. Congressman Schiff who was the lead House manager in the trial gave a very emotional and rational closing:

"We must say enough, enough! He has betrayed our national security, and he will do so again. He has compromised our elections, and he will do so again. You will not change him. You cannot constrain him. He is who he is. Truth matters little to him. What's right matters even less, and

decency matters not at all. Can we be confident that he will not continue to cheat in this very election? Can we be confident that Americans and not foreign powers will get to decide, and that the president will shun any further foreign interferencein our Democratic affairs? The short, plain, sad, incontestable answer is no, you can't. You can't trust this president to do the right thing. Not for one minute, not for one election, not for the sake of our country. You just can't. He will not change and you know it. What are the odds if left in office that he will continue trying to cheat? I will tell you: 100%. A man without character or ethical compass will never find his way."

Strong words and words that will be in the history books. Unfortunately his words fell on deaf ears and the country would see it come true.

The vote was strictly along party lines with one exception. Senator Romney did break with the party on the abuse of power charge and voted guilty, but he voted not guilty on the obstruction of Congress charge. So Trump got away twice now, first on the Mueller Report and now on the impeachment charges. Just like Teflon, nothing sticks.

The primary election process begins

Trump informally launched his bid for reelection February 2017. When the GOP really started the primary process, there were really only three serious opponents, Bill Weld, former Massachusetts governor, Joe Walsh, former congressman from Illinois, and Mark Sanford, former governor and congressman from South Carolina. The RNC in February 2019 voted to provide undivided support to Trump. Sanford would withdraw in November 2019, Walsh withdrew February 2020, and Weld withdrew March 2020. Because of Covid, several states would postpone their primaries or caucuses and others continued voting in person. Because of Trump's claims about fraud related to voting by mail, it discouraged the expansion and promotion of such voting during the GOP primary. Trump won the primary with over 18 million votes, the most ever for an incumbent president.

He was definitely emboldened by the results in the Senate trial. He didn't know for sure who he might be running against but it didn't really matter. He immediately started planting the seeds of doubt, stating that if he didn't win the general election it would have to be rigged. Don't forget that it worked during the GOP primary in 2016. He once again bragged about his accomplishments, most of which were exaggerations or out and out lies. It really didn't matter though, because the GOP elected to not even bother to have a new platform to run on. Instead they pledged to "enthusiastically" support him and his America first agenda.

It would be interesting to see who the Democrats would run against him and how the general election would work with the ongoing pandemic.

My view point

It's obvious that I wasn't a Trump supporter. I was still a Republican hoping that the country and the party would come to their senses. Up until this time, the party had survived the Nixon crisis and the George W. Bush win by the Supreme Court, all of which to me paled compared to what we were experiencing now. What happened to all the Regan Republicans? Why wasn't the party speaking up and calling out what they knew was wrong?

Friends of mine that had supported Trump were beginning to question their votes in the 2016 election, but there were still many who would stand by Trump and his actions. I felt that the country was approaching a crossroad of keeping our democracy or possibly falling victim to an autocrat. Trump would go on to pardon those people who supported him with their lies and actions that were a danger to our country. Roger Stone, Michael Flynn, Steve Bannon, and Paul Manafort were all pardoned.

His lies and exaggerations about Covid-19 politicized the pandemic that was killing Americans, ruining the economy and was deepening the division of our country. The threat of radicalization was in the air. I could only hope that he wouldn't get re-elected and at the same time I feared what could be coming no matter the results.

CHAPTER 15

Joe Biden, Democrat, January 2021 – Present

There was no doubt in my mind that the 2020 Democrat presidential primary would be something else. I really was concerned that the Democrats would end up with some radical version of a candidate that would once again turn voters off. Surely they wouldn't put Hillary Clinton up for consideration, would they?

Clinton didn't try again, but there were 29 people trying for the nomination. It was a real cross-section of the demographics of America. Six women were running, one openly gay man, one Latino, one Asian-American, several African-Americans, a billionaire, a stated Socialist Democrat, a former Vice-President, quite a few governors, senators, representatives, a couple of mayors, businessmen with no political experience, and a writer. There were more Democrat candidates running then since the inception of the modern primary system. I counted 12 that would withdraw before 2019 was over.

Their ideologies were as diversified as their backgrounds. Some were rather extreme left in their thinking and there were also quite a few that were moderates.

The Democrats started their process before Covid. They scheduled 12 televised debates, but only had 11 cancelling the final debate when it became evident who the winner would be. Of the 29 candidates, 23 were in at least one debate. Only Biden and Sanders would be in all 11 debates. Pete Buttigieg, Amy Klobuchar, and Elizabeth Warren would be in all but one. With so many people there was going to be some fireworks about the debates. The first debate ran for two days, June 26 – 27, 2019. Who would participate on what date was determined by drawing lots. Biden drew the second day's appearance. He didn't do well. Senator Kamala Harris attacked him on his past comments on being able to work with segregationist Senators when he was in the Senate and his stance on desegregation busing. He was so caught off guard by the attack that he looked like a fish out of water.

The second debate turned into a real clash between the liberal and moderate candidates. These people were really far apart ideologically.

The whole debate process was a continuous dispute over the handling and qualifications necessary to be in the debates and claims that microphones were being turned off for certain candidates. One of the candidates, Michael Bloomberg, was self-funding his run. He was disqualified for a period of time from the debates do to a requirement that you had to have had a certain percentage of your money donated. The billionaire didn't need any donations.

By the time the 9th debate rolled around, February 19, 2020, there were only six candidates left, Elizabeth Warren, Amy Klobuchar, Bernie Sanders, Pete Buttigieg, Michael Bloomberg, and Joe Biden. It is said that it was the most watched Democrat debate of all time with over 19.7 million viewers.

The Primary Election

The Democrat primaries ran from February 3 to August 20th. Traditionally the first three states having their primary would tell the story of who would be in the winner's circle. In Iowa, Pete Buttigieg would win the Caucus with Bernie Sanders coming in second place. In New Hampshire, Bernie Sanders won with a narrow victory over Buttigieg. Sanders also won Nevada. Where was Biden? He lost in all three and it looked like he might be out of the running early. There was one hope and one hope only and that was the South Carolina primary. Representative Jim Clyburn was the leading Democrat for South Carolina and motivated the African American voters. He endorsed Joe Biden who won the state and 10 out of 15 states on Super Tuesday. When Biden became the presumptive winner of the nomination Bernie Sanders withdrew. On August 11th, Biden announced that Kamala Harris would be his running mate.

Democrat Platform

The Democrats had their convention scheduled in Milwaukee, Wisconsin. Due to the Covid pandemic this wasn't going to be the big show that conventions normally are. A good part of the convention was conducted remotely and that included the drafting of the Democrat Platform. Political platforms can get pretty wordy maybe 60 plus pages. Fortunately Sydney Ember and Matt Stevens wrote an article for the New Your Times that was published August 19, 2020 that highlighted the most important items. The platform addressed the Coronavirus pandemic supporting increased funding for the CDC, providing more aid to state and local governments for things such as contact tracing, free coronavirus testing and treatment for everyone and free vaccines when they become available. On general healthcare the Democrats wanted to bring down the costs of prescription drugs, reduce healthcare costs, and seek universal health care through a public option, but not Medicare for all.

On the economy they wanted to raise the minimum wage to $15 an hour, invest in infrastructure, and encourage home ownership by increasing affordable housing and giving a $15,000 tax credit to first-time home buyers.

The platform also promised to "reject every effort to cut, privatize, or weaken Social Security.

The platform also addressed climate change with a goal of eliminating carbon pollution from power plants by 2035 and achieving net-zero greenhouse emissions by 2050.

The Democrats also supported statehood for Washington DC and a path to citizenship for undocumented immigrants.

Regarding criminal justice and racial justice the platform does not support defunding the police. It does however support a national standard governing the use of force banning things like chokeholds. It also wanted to eliminate cash bail, decriminalize marijuana and legalize for medical use, but leave it up to the states whether they wanted to legalize recreational use.

In support of education, the platform supports making public colleges and universities tuition-free for students whose families make less than $125,000 and supports making community colleges and trade schools tuition free for all students. It also wanted to ban for profit private charter schools from receiving federal funding.

In the foreign policy arena it supports a two state solution that would establish an independent Palestinian state and that Jerusalem should remain the capital of Israel.

Now what was the GOP platform? Oh yeah, there wasn't one.

THE GENERAL ELECTION BIDEN VS. TRUMP

I thought it was pretty obvious that with the Covid pandemic that the normal methods of campaigns in the past and voting when the time came, might be affected. Here's a quick look at both candidates:

Trump campaign:

Even Trump was sort of avoiding massive gatherings at first as recommended by the CDC and actually prohibited in many cities and states. The turning point though occurred in June. A CNN poll showed that Trump was 14 points behind Biden. He decided to resume rallies. His first was in Tulsa, OK. As usual he and his campaign exaggerated about the numbers. The campaign claimed that one million tickets had been requested for the Tulsa rally. The rally was scheduled at the Bank of Oklahoma Center. The Center has a seating capacity of only 19,199. The Tulsa fire department ever watchful of capacity at events in case of fire, estimated that less than 6200 had attended. I watched it on television and it looked like a lot of empty seats to me. Of course hardly anyone wore masks. Trump spent the first 14 minutes talking about his visit to West Point and the pictures and comments regarding him walking down a ramp. Quite a few attendees came down with Covid, including Herman Cain who died 4 weeks later from Covid. It was covered on the news that Trump was really upset over the attendance and was upset with his campaign manager.

Further rallies were held in Phoenix and Yuma, AZ. Turnout was nothing like he had during his first run for president. July 4th Trump held a rally at Mt

Rushmore. The governor gave him a small replica of the Presidents on Mt Rushmore, which showed his face on it. Once again, **his speech highlighted that the vote would be rigged by mail-in ballots**. Interesting was that was also the same day that Kayne West announced that he was going to run for president. It was believed it was just an effort to try to pull Black voters from Biden.

Later in the month during a Fox News Interview Trump called their network poll that showed Biden leading by 8 points "fake". Asked if he would accept losing, he replied he "would have to see" **citing mail-in ballots would be rigged against him**.

Trump's campaign liked to try to compare him to Reagan especially for fund raising. They had a coin they would sell you that showed Reagan and Trump together. Finally in July the Reagan Foundation and Institute had enough and formally asked the campaign and the RNC to stop using the Reagan name and likeness for fund raising.

July 23rd Trump cancelled the Jacksonville portion of the RNC convention due to rising Covid numbers. A week later he suggested delaying the election due to Covid. He didn't seem to understand only Congress can make such a change. He finally walks that idea back and then **condemns mail-in voting again.** It was also reported that at that time, by supposedly high ranking members of the GOP, that Mitch McConnell signaled GOP candidates that they may distance themselves from Trump if it will help them with their own campaign. Maybe someone saw the writing on the wall?

Come September, Trump told a television station in Wilmington, NC, that **people should vote twice, once in person and again by mail** to see if anyone stops them from committing an illegal act. CNN asked AG Bill Barr about this statement and Barr claimed he didn't know whether it was illegal to vote twice. Huh?

Campaigning in Pennsylvania, Trump encouraged voters to vote in person, referencing **potential mail fraud or ballots going missing.** This kind of campaigning upset many in the GOP who felt that with the pandemic going on voting by mail would be a major player in the election to avoid potential exposure to the disease.

Trump was asked again during a press conference that month if he would commit to a peaceful transition of power if he lost. He replied, "Well, we'll have to see what happens.

I've been complaining very strongly about the ballots. And the ballots are a disaster. Get rid of the ballots and you'll have a very peaceful – there won't be a transfer, frankly. There will be a continuation". He also said it was important for his nominee to the Supreme Court be confirmed as he believed the election would be settled there. It sounded to me like he didn't expect to win and why was he saying what he was saying about the ballots when the election hadn't even taken place yet? Also troubling was that his son, Don Jr., posted that he was asking "able-bodied" people to join an election security "army" for his father. A what? That sounded like more than just official Poll Watchers which is common in elections.

Biden campaign:

Joe Biden's campaign really had two major parts to take care of if he was to win the election. The first part was uniting the Democrat Party. There was a gap between the moderates and the left wing of the party. Thanks to Bernie Sanders working with Biden to bridge the gap the party finally came together, even though many of the left wing were not happy. The second part was getting the word out to the voters why they should elect him.

Unlike Trump who was holding large rallies, Biden targeted when he would go on the road and how rallies would be held. He stuck with what the health experts were saying about large gatherings. He did a lot of virtual campaigning from his home. When he was out, his gatherings observed social distancing between attendees. He also wore a mask and his audience was masked. He really believed that having massive crowds during the pandemic wasn't appropriate. I remember one event that he held in Florida that was televised that must have been a first in political campaigning. The event was a drive-in. People actually sat in the cars for the entire presentation he gave blowing their horns rather than applauding.

Trump attacked Biden for not being out like he was doing, but voters seemed to accept Biden's method with full understanding of why his campaign was conducted as it was. It was really different and I wondered at the time how successful it would be.

Because Trump was his own worst enemy during his administration and his attempt to win another term a large number of Republicans came out and gave their support publicly to Biden. Former staffers of Senator Mitt Romney, President George W. Bush, Senator John McCain and 25 former Republican congressional members, endorsed Biden. Additionally, 175 current and former law enforcement officials, 780 retired generals, admirals, senior non-commissioned officers, ambassadors, and national security officials signed a letter endorsing Biden. As a lifelong Republican at the time, I don't think I could remember anything like that happening before.

The debates:

What's a presidential election without debates? There were three debates scheduled.

The first debate was moderated by Chris Wallace of Fox News. The subjects to cover were both candidate's records, the economy, the pandemic, race relations, and the Supreme Court nominee. The rules were fairly simple. Each candidate would have 2 minutes to give their position followed by a discussion. The audience in attendance were to wear masks during the entire debate. Trump's family refused masking. Once the debate started, the rules were out the window. Quickly it turned into cross talk and interruptions. Trump would interrupt Biden and Wallace, and when Wallace asked many times for Trump to follow the rules, he was ignored. It reminded me of when Trump ran against Clinton and how he would walk up behind her when she was talking, trying to intimidate her. I thought several times that the debate could become physical. When Biden challenged Trump to condemn white nationalist, Trump wanted Biden to give him a name of a group. Biden said how about the Proud Boys? Trump refused to condemn them or any other group. **Instead he said to the Proud Boys, "Stand back and standby"**. That remark would come back to haunt him. Then he urged his supporters to "go into the polls and watch very carefully because that's what has to happen".

The second debate was to take place October 15th. It was cancelled. Covid-19 had struck the White House. Trump had tweeted that he and the First Lady had both tested positive and would go into quarantine. The campaign cancelled all in-person events scheduled. Trump also refused to participate in a virtual debate with Biden. Both ended up doing separate Town Hall speeches instead.

The third and final debate place on October 22nd. Kristen Welker of NBC was the moderator. To prevent the childish show they happened during the first debate, the microphones of the candidates were muted when it wasn't their turn to talk. Trump was pushing Biden as to why his 2020 campaign promises weren't delivered during his eight years as Vice-President. Biden famously responded, "We had a Republican Congress".

Danger signs

There was a dangerous occurrence a little over a week after the debates. A Biden campaign bus travelling from San Antonio, TX to Austin, TX on I-35 was followed and harassed by several vehicles, almost causing an accident. The bus was carrying a former State Senator and campaign staff. The drivers of the vehicles were flying Trump flags. The Biden campaign cancelled two scheduled events in Austin as a result of this action.

The FBI investigated the incident. Trump criticized the FBI for doing so and tweeted, "**In my opinion, these patriots did nothing wrong**. Instead the FBI and Justice should be investigation the terrorist, anarchists, and agitators of ANTIFA, who run around burning down our Democrat run cities and hurting our people!"

Election Day!

It finally arrived. Time to go cast my vote. My wife like so many other Americans had elected to vote by mail because of the pandemic. Not me. I put on my mask and walked across the street to my polling place and stood in line with a bunch of other people for over an hour. First time I ever had to wait that long to vote.

This would be a historical year for voting. Nationwide over 155 million citizens would vote. Many states had expanded their early voting periods, increased mail-in voting and overall access to means of being able to cast their ballots safely due to the pandemic.

Every state has their own rules on voting including the counting of ballots. Most generally mail-in ballots and sometimes the early voting ballots are not counted until after the polls close and sometimes not until the following day. We have become rather spoiled by the media with them making projections of who has won what states even before all the votes have been counted. So when the tabulation is being accomplished what you see on television isn't the actual totals. Historically, Democrats have voted more often by mail and Republicans have voted more often in person. This can lead to some misunderstanding of who is winning or who has won way too early. Early reporting made it seem that Trump was in the lead then it started changing. It started looking like he had loss by late evening. Even his staff was reading it that way. Needless to say he was pretty pissed. It has been reported that Rudy Giuliani encouraged him to go and announce himself as the winner, even though the count was far from over. He did and of course exaggerated how much he had won by. On November 7th CNN, ABC News, CBS, Fox News, Reuters, Associate Press, and the New York Times, would project that Biden had won. When all the states certified their election results, I hoped that the four years of craziness was over. I was to be disappointed. We were heading into a major threat to our country and democracy.

After Election Day problems

When the final count was accomplished and certified, Biden had over 81 million popular votes and Trump had a little over 74 million votes. Biden would get 304 of the Electoral College votes and Trump 232, pretty cut and dry, except Trump wouldn't concede the election. He and his supporters challenged the election claiming fraud and all kinds of off the wall things. Election challenges are normal but this was really getting crazy. Even the administrator of the GSA refused to authorize transition funds until November 23rd which would hinder the Biden team from getting the new administration started. Trump's people went to court 61 times and lost 60 times their challenges and it was many times in front of Republican elected judges. Despite his White House attorney's and AG Bill Barr assurances of no proof of fraud that could change the results of the election, Trump still wouldn't concede. Instead of following the traditional and legally required actions for a peaceful transition of power, the administration did all they could to obstruct. If the legal actions didn't produce the desired result for the President, maybe other actions would. He reached out to the swing states wanting their support to invalidate the election counts in their states and recount the votes.

Trump and his right wing supporters and media started tweeting and using podcasts to push his false election stolen stories pretty hard in December. Pro-Trump rallies were held in D.C. called "Stop the Steal" rallies. He tweeted on the 19th, that it was "statistically impossible to have lost the 2020 Election. **Big protest in D.C. on January 6th. Be there, will be wild!"** What was important about the date? That is when the Electoral College Votes would be certified by the Vice-President. Again on the 26th he tweeted criticism of the Justice Department and the FBI and reminded everyone of the January 6th protest. On the 27th he tweeted again a reminder of January 6th, January 1st, he tweeted twice regarding the BIG Protest Rally in Washington, DC, on January 6th, Stop the Steal! On January 3rd he retweeted @CodeMonkeyZ: "If you are planning to attend peaceful protests in DC on the 6th, I recommend wearing a body camera. The more video angles of that day the better". January 4th, in Georgia for the Senate runoffs, Trump said, "If the liberal Democrats take the Senate and the White House – and they're not taking this White House – **we're going to fight like hell, I'll tell you right now, we're going to take it back".**

As if his tweets and speeches weren't bad enough, on January 2, 2021, Trump made his infamous phone call to the Georgia Secretary of State, Brad Raffensperger, trying to pressure him to change the vote count in Georgia. The phone call was being recorded and would be used in his next impeachment as evidence.

Meanwhile Trump's supporters supposedly under the direction of Rudy Giuliani and his team, were illegally setting up self-declared "alternate electors" and phony documents to overturn their states results and give their votes to Trump.

The Trump White House was trying to convince the Vice-President that he had the power to declare the ballots received for certification null and void and throw out the results and have Congress make the Presidential selection. He tried to bully the VP and it didn't work. Vice-President Pence after seeking legal advice, told Trump that he didn't have that authority.

On January 5th, Steve Bannon in a podcast basically told the world what was going to happen the next day. January 6th would be the day of reckoning. It just blew my mind how people were saying they were taken by surprise. If I could see back before the election and definitely after the election that something was brewing, why didn't the professionals in law enforcement and the media catch on? The Capitol was stormed by rioters and militias. People would die that day. The crowd was looking for members of Congress and the Vice-President. They were chanting, "Hang Mike Pence" is response to a Trump tweet that the VP wouldn't do what he wanted him to do. Late that night after reinforcements from the National Guard and DC police arrived, the count would resume and Biden would be President-Elect scheduled to be sworn in on January 20th. Trump would face a second impeachment, the first time in US history.

The Second Impeachment

It didn't matter which political party you belonged to for when the Capitol was breached, everyone was in danger. The country was lucky that we didn't have a slaughter of Congress and the Vice-President. Understandably when it was all over both parties and both houses were shook up. House Minority Leader Kevin McCarthy and Senator Minority Leader McConnell both rebuked Trump publicly. Maybe the GOP, **the party of law and order** was finally going to stand up. One week before his term in office would expire, the House impeached him for incitement of insurrection and lawless action at the Capitol. Only ten Republican representatives voted to impeach, Representatives Kato, Kinzinger, Cheney, Upton, Beutler, Newhouse, Meijer, Rice, Gonzalez, and Valadao. The most ever from a president's party. The impeachment went to the Senate in February after Trump left office. During the vote 57 Senators voted guilty, including Republican Senators, Burr, Cassidy, Collins, Murkowski, Romney, Sasse, and Toomey. Not enough to convict.

Why did they even bother knowing he would be out of office even before the Senate trial? Mainly, it was to hold him accountable and show no one is above the law and hope a conviction would remove him from any future consideration for the Presidency or any public office. Sadly, my Republican Party, chickened out afraid of being voted out of office by Trump supporters in the future. The Teflon President escaped again. That's when I decided to leave the Republican Party.

Inauguration Day – Biden is sworn in as President

I think I heard a loud sigh of relief when Biden was sworn in as President. Somehow we survived the January 6th insurrection, at least temporarily, and the country had to keep its guard up on inauguration day as there were threats of action being taken against the event in D.C. and state capitols. Trump would not attend as was normal in past inaugurations. Outgoing Vice President Pence was in attendance, along with Senators Shumer and McConnell, Speaker of the House Pelosi, and House Minority Leader McCarthy. All in attendance had to wear masks, pass Covid testing, temperature check, and maintain social distancing. Physical security was wrapped up with 25,000 National Guard troops, and law enforcement. The entire area was surrounded by high fencing with razor wire on top.

The inauguration was unlike what we were used to seeing. With the pandemic in full swing we didn't see the crowd that is generally present for the event. All events including traditional entertainment was livestreamed.

Biden's speech was relatively short projecting a vision to unite the nation and return to a familiar normalcy. He addressed the pandemic, the economy, climate change, racial injustice, and the political polarization in the country. He pledged that we would engage with the world again, and repair our alliances. A large number of foreign leaders applauded his speech. They felt America was back.   He also promised to "always level" with the American public and govern in their interests. He was very convincing.

I think that Biden is basically a good man with a tremendous amount of experience in government. As a Senator he was known for being able to work across the aisle. He was also known for having many Republican friends. Unlike many in Congress, he maintained contact with his constituents even going so far to take the AMTRAC home to Delaware every day. His background was quite similar to many of us, coming from a working class family. It was easy to identify with him. He had a history of overcoming personal problems such as his stuttering as a kid and suffering the tragedy of losing his wife and daughter in a car wreck and then raising his boys following the accident. He suffered through the loss of a son to cancer. He was humble but wasn't afraid to speak out when he thought something was wrong. All outstanding traits to have in a President. He has one weakness though. He still believes that both parties can work together and that doesn't seem true anymore. I felt he was going to have a "hard row to hoe".

The Democrats had the majority in the House and Senate, but a very slim majority. The Senate was split 50-50. With the Vice President's vote being able to break any ties, but if the Republicans decided to filibuster, they could hold up or prevent a lot of legislation and don't forget the obstructionist attitude during the Obama administration. Even the Democrats themselves have some division within their own ranks which would make life tough for the new President.

The First Year and Challenges

Just like any other President new to the office he had some promises to keep. According to Wikipedia, using Executive Orders during his first quarter, he addressed several things:

1. Rescinded the US withdraw from the World Health Organization
2. Revoked the Trump's executive order regarding the Keystone XL pipeline
3. Put a hold on the funding for Trump's wall
4. Repealed the travel ban from Muslim majority nations
5. Extended the pause on Federal student loan payments
6. Took action on the Covid-19 response and vaccination efforts
7. Activated the Defense Production act for distributing vaccines
8. Boosted food aid and stimulus check delivery

9. Restored collective bargaining for federal employees
10. Increased the minimum wage for federal employees to $15 hourly
11. Repelled the ban on transgender members in the military
12. Suspended new natural gas and oil leases on federal land and waters as part of his climate program.
13. Expanded the Affordable Care Act and Medicaid
14. Ordered the reuniting of illegal immigrant kids with their families
15. Extended the foreclosure ban and forbearance thru June
16. Reverted the citizenship test back to the 2008 version
17. Reversed the ban on permanent residency "green cards" to immigrants
18. Signed order promoting voter rights

Now you don't have to agree with everything he did, but he accomplished with executive orders, what many in the country wanted done. The problem with executive orders is that they aren't law. The next guy in office can reverse them and sometimes if they are challenged in court and they can be over ruled by the court.

Biden took on the most pressing problem at the time which was the pandemic. He gave Trump credit for Operation Warp Speed, but the Biden administration had the challenge of getting people vaccinated to protect lives and get the country back on the road to recovery. He set realistic goals for vaccinations and his administration exceeded those goals every month. Even though there was a tremendous effort to educate people on why they should get vaccinated there were still many who wouldn't do so. They fell victim to anti-vax propaganda, wouldn't wear masks, and slowed down getting the country open again. When the administration pushed industries and the federal government to make mandatory vaccinations there was an uproar. This would eventually end up in federal court for a decision.

He did push for the Senate resolution of a $1.9 billion stimulus package. He extended the Paycheck Protection Program until the end of May and he signed the American Rescue Plan into law. Pretty busy for his first quarter in office. His handling of the pandemic resulted in the highest approval rating of his presidency.

His **second quarter** was primarily spent selling his programs across the country, but there were some other issues. The administration announced the intention to make a full withdrawal of American forces from Afghanistan by September 11th. The meaning of the date wasn't lost on me, but I kind of cringed that it was publicly announced. That just meant the Taliban could plan their actions based on our announced date.

Biden was active on the international scene. He met with the G7, NATO, and Putin. I'm sure the meeting with Putin wasn't the friendliest. We had just sanctioned Russia over a cyber-attack against us. He also revoked the "Remain in Mexico" policy. However the federal courts eventually forced re-instatement of the policy.

Covid was still a problem. A new variant was identified and became dominant. The CDC did lift the masking requirement for the fully vaccinate in most situations, but by the end of the quarter over 600,000 Americans had died from the disease.

By the 3rd quarter Biden's approval rating reportedly dropped to 43%. What brought that on? For one thing the economy was in trouble. Because of Covid our supply chain was in trouble driving prices up. Many businesses, especially the service industry had shut down and never reopened. Many people were either working from home or not working at all. Things were starting to loosen up some but not quick enough.

I think Afghanistan had much to do with it his drop in approval ratings. The Taliban was actively fighting and even though their actions weren't directed at our military by agreement, they were kicking butt. Biden ordered a B-52 strike against them. Then the Afghan government fell quicker than expected. There was an evacuation ordered of all Americans. Even though they had been warned early to get out of country, many ignored the order. It was total chaos. As the Taliban took over the capitol thousands of Afghans fled to the airport trying to leave as were many Americans who got cut off from escape. It was all televised. It reminded me of the evacuation of Saigon. We had to send more troops in to protect the evacuation and we lost people. Twelve marines and a navy medic died in an explosion by a suicide bomber at the airport. The last C-17 lifted off on August 30th. Over 122,000 were evacuated. Attempts are still being made to sneak out Afghans that supported our troops during the 20 years of warfare.

There are many veterans that are angry about the war and the way it ended. Many served several combat tours there and knew Afghans that supported us and felt that we left our allies behind. I understand. I just don't know though how else it could have ended. Military leaders for years have said there was no military solution. I do think the war was way too long. Our mission was to get Bin Laden and we did. Nation building sucked us in for too many years.

July 1st, largely along party-line vote, **the January 6th Committee** was formed to investigate the attack on the Capitol Building and the attempt to overturn the Electoral College vote count. Speaker Pelosi would be able to appoint eight members, of which one was Republican Liz Cheney, and Minority Leader McCarthy could appoint five members, with approval by Pelosi. He recommended Republican Representatives, Jim Banks, Jim Jordan, Rodney Davis, Kelly Armstrong, and Troy Nehls. Jordan, Nehls, and

Banks had voted to overturn the Electoral College votes of Pennsylvania and Arizona. Additionally Jordan and Banks had also supported the invalidation of the ballots of voters in four states. **Pelosi rejected Banks and Jordan but accepted the other three recommendations**. McCarthy then pulled all of his candidates and said he wouldn't recommend anyone unless his five were approved. Pelosi then appointed Republican Adam Kinzinger to the committee along with several GOP advisors and lawyers to support the committee's investigation and give it a bipartisan look. The RNC censured Cheney and Kinzinger for being on the committee. At the time of this writing the committee's hearings are still on going. The televised hearings had Republicans as witnesses and the illegal activities involving Trump supporters, in and out of the government were made crystal clear.

As usual "mother nature" was wreaking havoc. Hurricane Ida hit Louisiana causing major damage and in the west, especially California, fires were raging. The scientist claimed climate change was the culprit behind both.

The Democrats were having some problems getting things accomplished in the Senate. The filibuster rule was hampering everything. There was talk of using the "Nuclear Option" to eliminate the filibuster just as the GOP did during the Obama administration, but President Biden opposed the idea.

The fourth quarter would be critical. Biden warned in October that the government would breach its $28.4 trillion debt limit in historic default if both parties don't vote on the infrastructure bill. **Come November he would sign a bipartisan infrastructure bill**. This was the first time in decades that something was finally accomplished on infrastructure. His predecessor spoke about it many times but never took action. A $1 Trillion package (over a 5 year period) was signed by the Biden. This was a real bi-partisan law supported by 19 GOP Senators and 13 GOP Representatives in the House. According to the White House website, www.whitehouse.gov , "This Bipartisan Infrastructure Law will rebuild America's roads, bridges and rails, expand access to clean drinking water, ensure every American has access to high-speed internet, tackle the climate crisis, advance environmental justice, and invest in communities that have too often been left behind. The legislation will help ease inflationary pressures and strengthen supply chains by making long overdue improvements for our nation's ports, airports, rail, and roads. It will drive the creation of good-paying union jobs and grow the economy sustainably and equitably so that everyone gets ahead for decades to come. Combined with the President's Build Back Framework, it will add on average 1.5 million job per year for the next 10 years."

I would say that at last something really big was accomplished by the President and Congress. Biden also extended the payment pause on student loans until May. Pretty big victories for the President and a great way to end his first year in office.

Not everything was good though. Gas prices were rising and he blamed OPEC for that. A Federal judge ruled against the vaccine mandate and Senator Manchin said he wouldn't support President Biden's climate and economic agenda.

The second year 2022

This would be a very difficult year. The divisions in the country were still growing. The attempt to pass the John Lewis Voting Rights Act would not happen in the Senate because of the filibuster rules and no one would take the action needed to make it happen. Various states started passing laws that would make voting harder, claiming that they were securing the election process. Some Republican controlled state legislatures were trying to change their laws to where they could decide who won elections rather than the voters. With this being a mid-term election year false stories of the election being stolen were firing up again by candidates being supported by Trump. Mass shootings were on the increase and lead to the increasing demand for some type of gun control. The Supreme Court would be making some very decisive decisions on issues that would rile the public up. Russia would invade Ukraine and turn the world upside down.

January we were still experiencing fires in the western part of the country. Wildfires had devastated parts of Colorado. Mid-month the Supreme Court blocked the workplace mandatory Covid vaccine mandate.

In **February** the GOP attacked and censured Representatives Kinzinger and Chaney for being on the January 6th Committee. Kinzinger had already announced that he wasn't running for re-election but Chaney was. The GOP and Trump went after her. If it wasn't bad enough that the party turned on her, both she and Kinzinger have had death threats against them and their families.

By mid-month NSA Jake Sullivan began warning of an imminent invasion of Ukraine by Russia. The administration responded by sending more troops to NATO. President Biden warned Putin of swift and severe costs if invasion took place. The administration kept warning the Ukrainian government but they weren't taking the warning seriously. On the 17th they warned the Ukrainians again that invasion was imminent. Putin claimed that neo-Nazis were persecuting the Russian minorities in Ukraine and on the 21st, he recognized the Donetsk People's Republic and the Luhansk People's Republic in eastern Ukraine as independent nations. They in turn requested Russian help. On the 24th Putin announced a "Special Military Operation" and the invasion began.

We didn't expect the Ukrainians to last more than a couple weeks at the most. The Russians attacked from several directions but the real effort was in the north with the idea of taking the Ukrainian capital and installing a new government. We had evacuated our embassy and had pulled out all US military trainers before it occurred. To everyone's surprise the Russians stalled and were getting pushed back. The US and NATO began increasing the supply of weapons and Poland and several other NATO countries opened their borders to refugees. Over 9.1 million people fled the country. It was the largest refugee crisis since WWII. The US provided $350 million in military aid.

In **March** President Biden submitted a plan to congress to provide $5.7 trillion in military and financial aid to Ukraine. I have no idea where that amount of money would come from. Sanctions were placed on Russia and their leaders. NATO and the US stepped up support to the Ukrainians with weapons and humanitarian aid. Europe upped their sanctions despite the fact they get most of their energy from Russia. One thing that was done to help calm our people and allies was that the US and NATO said no "boots on the ground!" Russia didn't get a quick victory as they and the world thought, but the war goes on.

The price of gasoline continued to rise. Some blame was placed on Russia but there are many reasons behind it. Biden started releasing 1 million barrels of oil from the strategic reserve per day. This was to continue for six months.

April was a continuation of the international problems in Ukraine but nationally the major highlights were the signing of the Postal Reform Act, which should help with the financial mess that the post offices have had for years because they were required to prefund their retirement program, and the confirmation of Ketanji Brown Jackson to the Supreme Court, the first black woman in history to be nominated and confirmed. Biden also asked congress for $33 billion in aid to Ukraine, including $20 billion in military aid. It would be approved and passed the following month with more than requested, upping the amount to $40 billion.

In **May** several things were turning the country upside down. We had been experiencing a shortage of baby formula. Apparently Abbott Labs had a plant in Sturgis, Michigan that produce a special type of baby formula. The formula had supposedly resulted in the death of several infants due to contamination. The lab had recalled the formula. The plant had been inspected in January and found to have problems that resulted in the shutdown of the plant. That coupled with the fact that there were restrictions on importing foreign made formula resulted in a serious shortage. How that was the fault of any President is beyond me, but the outrage was there. Biden ended up invoking the Defense Production Act for baby formula and imports were allowed. Even US aircraft were used to bring formula into the country.

A second major event was the leaking of a Supreme Court opinion that would end up overturning Roe vs Wade. The country went deeper into division. States would start invoking the harshest laws against abortions. Texas and others went so far as to criminalize abortions and threaten doctors and women with prison time. They were even considering anyone that contributed by given a women a ride to an abortion a criminal. Texas told citizens that they could sue anyone that had an abortion or contributed to an abortion basically having citizens act as bounty hunters enforcing state laws. These laws made no exceptions for rape or incest. Protest erupted all over the country. The fight is still going on and unless Congress passes an abortion law, the people are stuck with it. The GOP is paying a price as more women are registering as Democrats and many of the Republican women are not support Republicans running for office that don't support abortion rights.

The President made a comment, "This MAGA crowd is really the most extreme political organization that's existed in American history, in recent American history".

In **June** there were several mass shooting incidents again. The President pressed Congress to take some kind of action. The Senate and the House had different ideas on what should be done, but finally in the Senate some support came from Minority Leader McConnell and some advances were made but nothing really revolutionary. Despite calls for an assault weapons ban, a ban on high capacity magazines, and red flag laws it didn't happen. The Supreme Court ruled in favor of the NY Rifle Pistol Association, Inc vs Bruen that New York State laws that had been in effect for over 100 years were unconstitutional and couldn't keep people from carrying a concealed weapon unless licensed.

In Ukraine the Russians started gaining ground. This prompted the US and NATO to start provided more powerful and advanced rocket and missile systems resulting in Russia making threats against the West and talk of possibly nuclear war being on the horizon.

The Covid situation has worsened. Another new variant, BA.4 and BA.5, is spreading more easily and becoming the pre-dominate one. Over 1,018,035 Americans have now died from Covid. As of July 15th, according to the CDC, over 70 million Americans have not been vaccinated. Approximately only 28% of adults with the first booster have had a 2nd booster shot. Hospital and death rates for older adults have risen. Only 67% of the total population have been fully vaccinated and 50.2% of total booster eligible population has not received the first booster shot.

Biden finally had a big win in August. The Inflation Reduction Act was passed. Just how much inflation will be reduced is debatable but it did include some very important actions to occur over a ten year period, for instance prescription drug price reform to include Medicare negotiation of drug prices including a cap on insulin costs at $35 a month and a cap on out of pocket drug cost at $2000 for people on Medicare. It imposes a selective 15% corporate minimum tax rate for companies with higher than $1 billion of annual financial statement income, increases tax enforcement, and a 1% excise tax on stock buybacks.

Spending will include $369 billion towards energy security and climate change, $300 billion for deficit reduction, $64 billion for a three year extension of the Affordable Care Act subsidies, $4 billion in funding for drought resiliency in western states, and $80 billion in increased funding for IRS modernization and increased tax enforcement.

My take?

What else will occur before the end of the Biden administration? Who knows? With the mid-term elections coming up in the fall, the Democrats could lose control of both the House and Senate.

Trump is jeopardizing that opportunity for the GOP with his endorsements of MAGA Republican candidates that are still pushing radical views and that many party observers are describing as the worst candidates ever. Mainstream Republicans are losing in the primaries. Even Mitch McConnell is saying that he doesn't think they can win the majority in the Senate and maybe only a small majority in the House.

Trump has gotten in possible trouble with the DOJ for having classified documents and other government papers at his home in Florida. With the exception of the MAGA Republicans, he is running off mainstream Republican voters with his rhetoric.

Biden is on the campaign trail and is calling out the MAGA Republicans as a danger to our democracy. He seems to be firing up the Democrat base and Independent voters and his approval ratings are improving. There are many mainstream Republicans that are endorsing Democrats at the state level. I think the mid-term elections will tell the story of whether our democracy will continue or possibly fall.

CHAPTER 16

So America Are We In Trouble?

I think we are at a dangerous crossroads and if we make the wrong decisions and follow the wrong people, America will never be the same again. It is 1 minute to mid-night and our freedom and that of our children and grandchildren is on line. No one should be surprised as we were warned early in our history by leaders such as President George Washington, Jefferson, Madison, Hamilton, and Abraham Lincoln of the danger.

I am not a civics teacher or history teacher, but since we don't seem to mandatorily teach the subjects in school anymore please let me voice my observations and experiences.

There have always been political extremist and there always will be. Whether you are talking about conservatives or liberals, both political viewpoints have their nut cases. In a democracy it is finding the middle ground in viewpoints that holds everything together. We realized that at the founding of our country. Thirteen colonies (actually they thought of themselves as 13 different countries) came together to build one nation of free people, but they struggled to do it.

They started with the Articles of Confederation and it didn't take long to realize that wasn't going to work if you were going to have a functional National Government and finally the Constitution was written and agreed to. It wasn't perfect and that's why it was designed so that it could always be amended with the consent of the States to strengthen it and protect the citizen's rights to freedom. It didn't give rights to everyone when written. We still had slavery. Women couldn't vote. Native Americans couldn't vote and weren't even recognized as citizens. If you weren't white and a landowner you couldn't vote and it took centuries and a civil war to make improvements and we still have a lot of work to do.

Hopefully you know, even though surveys have shown most Americans don't, that there are three branches of government. The Legislative Branch (Congress), the Executive Branch (President), and the Judicial Branch (Supreme Court). By the Constitution these are separate, but equal entities, designed so that no particular branch can get out of control and ignore the other two.

Congress

Only Congress by the Constitution can make laws, declare war, and tax the people. It is the most important part of our government because it is to directly represent the wishes of the citizens, that's why it is addressed first in the Constitution. Every two years all the Representatives in the House are up for re-election. Theoretically you could have a complete turnover of the representatives. There is no limit to how many terms they can serve.

I think one mistake made when the Constitution was written, was the establishment of the second part of Congress, the Senate. The Senate was established because the smaller populated states were concerned that the larger populated states with the majority of citizens, would make all the laws without them. So with a Senate **(at the time Senators were appointed by the powers in a state, not elected),** the smaller states could possibly stop whatever the majority in the House (elected Representatives) might pass. Why is that a problem? It meant that those with power who appointed the Senators could overcome whatever the majority of their people wanted by telling their Senator to simply vote against what passed in the House of Representatives. Not exactly how democracy is supposed to work. Also Senators would serve for initially six years with 1/3 up for election every two years. There is no limit to how many terms they can serve. We did eventually pass the 17th amendment, April 1913, to the Constitution to where Senators would be elected by popular vote to office. I'm not sure that fixed the problem.

According to an **article written by columnist Eric Black, February 19, 2021 in the Minnesota News,** "the currently 50-50 Senate is divided among Party lines with two Independents caucusing with the Democrats. If you add up the population of states and assign half to each of their two senators, the Democratic half of the Senate represents 41,549,808 more people than the Republican half. This is because Republicans do much better in lower population states (majority white) and Democrats do better in higher population states (more diversified). For instance, Wyoming, with 579,000 residents, has two senators, as does California, with 39.5 million (a bit over 68 times more) residents. Wyoming regularly sends two Republicans to the Senate and California sends two Democrats." This means the folks in Wyoming with the smaller population have the same power and say so, as the folks in California with the much larger population. Is that fair? I bet you don't think so if you live in

California. The kicker is nothing can become federal law unless it passes the Senate. The Senate operates under different rules than the House. Even though by the Constitution a simple majority can pass a law in the Senate, under Senate rules it takes 60 votes to proceed to vote on a bill. This is where the filibuster kicks in. The rule can be overturned by a simple majority, but nowadays the minority party generally objects to overturning the rule which empowers them to obstruct what the other party is trying to pass and in the case of the current Senate, the majority party with the Vice-President being the tiebreaking vote, doesn't want to overturn the rule in case they are no longer the majority after the next election, no matter how the majority of Americans may feel about the issue. Smaller populated states have an advantage in the Senate. As an example, in March 2013, 62 senators represented about ¼ of the people in the United States. **That is minority control.**

An article in **The Intellectualist, by Jake Thomas, written February 6, 2020** was an interesting analysis. It stated that 18% of the US population elects 52% of the country's Senators. It was also noted in Vox that more than half of the U.S.

population now lives in just 9 states meaning that just 18 Senators represent the largest swathe of the country. It also referenced a University of Virginia analysis of census projections that by 2040 just eight states will be home to half of our population and about 70% of the population will live in 16 states. That means 30% of the population will control 68% of the Senate. Once again traditionally the Democrats hold the majority in the most populous states and the Republicans are the majority in the least populous states where white voters tend to be the majority of residents. An interesting statement in the article was, "The old school notion that malapportionment protects smaller states from a **"tyranny of the majority"** no longer holds, according to Vox, because "there's no reason to believe that residents of small states, as a class, make up a coherent interest group whose political concerns are in tension with residents of large states." The article went on to state, "The implications are many, but one point Vox made was that of the courts: "Two years ago, Neil Gorsuch made history, becoming the first member of the Supreme Court in American history to be nominated by a president who lost the popular vote and confirmed by a bloc of senators who represent less than half of the country. The second was Brett Kavanaugh." Of course there would be a third appointed the same way, Justice Amy Barrett, since that article was written. Something to think about. Just the President and the Senate have all this power and if we have a traditional bottleneck in congress it is generally in the Senate and these 100 people get elected for at least six years and have the final say so on who sits on the Judiciary for the rest of their lifetime.

Unfortunately over time Congress has handed more of their responsibility to the Executive branch and that has caused a lot of our problems. Vietnam is a good example where we fought a war that wasn't declared by congress who by the Constitution are the ones with the power to declare war. Another example are the **rules set up by executive branch agencies that are enforced as laws rather than laws passed by Congress.** The idea of a democracy is that the power is to remain with the people which is where Congress gets the okay to approve whatever it is the government is going to do, not with any one individual.

Executive

We have got to get over this idea that the President is God on earth. He is the Chief Executive Officer of the government. His powers are to be limited, otherwise you can easily end up with a Hitler, Stalin, Putin, or some other dictator. He can issue Executive Orders, but even those can be challenged and when a President leaves office, the next President can do away with those executive orders of a previous President.

I understand how some people might think a President should be able to make a decision without congress. It would definitely be faster, but that is an autocratic government, not a democracy. It would allow one person to do a lot of horrible things affecting your life and you couldn't do anything about it.

The title of Commander-in-Chief gets thrown around an awful lot. We have had people running for office and had people say, "He will make a great Commander-in-Chief". That's the title given to the President when we go to war, not peacetime. That's when the President is given additional powers while we are at war and those powers go away when the war is over. It is dangerous to have a person in office that takes the title Commander-in-Chief as his primary and sole right. The tendency to use the military for his own desires can be too tempting. The President is to represent all of us and defend the Constitution, not a particular political party, personal interest, or any interest other than the American people as a whole.

Judicial

The Judicial Branch (Supreme Court and federal district courts) has one of the most important responsibilities in our democracy. It is to insure that what we do at the federal and state level is legal and according to the Constitution. Federal judges and the Supreme Court judges have to be non-partisan and when they are reviewing a case their personal feelings and prejudices on a subject have to be put aside. They are to make decisions based solely on the Constitution. They don't make the law. They interpret the law based on the Constitution and legal history. These are very serious positions. When there is a vacancy a person is nominated by the President with the advice and consent of the Senate appointed. We citizens have no control over who is in this branch of government. The appointment is for life. The only way they can be removed is if they are impeached or they elect to step down. We can't afford to have partisan politics involved. Most importantly they are to recognize that **NO ONE** is above the law, no President, no member of congress, no judge, no one. We are all equal citizens under the Constitution.

WE HAVE BEEN WARNED

In her book, **How Civil Wars Start**, Barbara F. Walter writes that "Madison and Hamilton believed that **if American democracy were to die, it would happen at the hands of a faction, not an outside adversary but a homegrown group ravenous for control.** Given a chance the leaders of such a faction "adverse to the rights of other citizens or to the permanent and aggregate interest of the community" would consolidate power and elevate their own interest over the public good. They saw the threat based on class, i.e. property owners seeking to concentrate power to protect their wealth and prevent redistribution. Separate but equal branches of government would counter this threat. They couldn't predict that the fractionalization they feared wouldn't be rooted in class but ethnic identity. All voters at the time were white men."

Words of Warning from Washington's Farewell

In his farewell address to congress in 1796 Washington warned us of potential dangers to our way of life by those who would try to ignore the Constitution. Washington stressed the importance of respecting the Constitution as the law and until amended everyone has a duty to follow the Constitution of the established government. He warned about political parties and how **they don't necessarily follow the will of the nation but their own minority self-interest wanting to dominate over their opposition, seek revenge and can lead to giving absolute power to an individual who will turn the power to his own advantage and personal elevation and the ruin of public liberty.**

He states about political parties, "**It serves always to distract the public councils and enfeeble the public administration. It agitates the community with ill-founded jealousies and false alarms, kindles the animosity of one part against another, forments occasionally riot and insurrection. It opens the door to foreign influence and corruption, which finds a facilitated access to the government itself**

through the channels of party passions. Thus the policy and will of one country are subjected to the policy and will of another. There is an opinion that parties in free countries are useful checks upon the administration of the government and serve to keep alive the spirit of liberty. This within certain limits is probably true and in governments of a monarchical cast, patriotism may look with indulgence, if not favor, upon the spirit of party. But in those of popular character, in governments purely elective, it is a spirit not to be encouraged. From their natural tendency, it is certain there will always be enough of the spirit for every salutary purpose. And there being **a constant danger of excess**, the effort ought to be by force of public opinion to mitigate and assuage it."

Washington went on to speak about the administration of government and the constitutional powers of the administrators: "It is important likewise, that the habits of thinking in a free country should inspire caution in those entrusted with its administration, to confine themselves within their respective constitutional spheres, avoiding the exercise of the powers of one department to encroach upon another. **The spirit of encroachment tends to consolidate the** powers of all the departments in one, and thus create, whatever the form of government, a real despotism. **A just estimate of that love of power, and proneness to abuse it, which predominates in the human heart, is sufficient to satisfy us of the truth of this position.** The necessity of reciprocal checks in the exercise of political power by dividing and distributing it into different depositories and constituting each the guardian of the public weal against invasions by the others, has been evinced by experiments ancient and modern; some of them in our country under our own eyes. To preserve them must be as necessary as to institute them. **If in the opinion of the people, the distribution or modification of the constitutional powers be in any particular wrong, let it be corrected by an amendment in the way the Constitution designates. But let there be no change by usurpation, for though this, in one instance may be the instrument of good, it is the customary weapon by which free governments are destroyed. The precedent must always greatly overbalance in permanent evil and partial or transient benefit which the use can at any time yield."**

To be a little more modern, author Dean Koontz in his novel **Quicksilver** wrote a paragraph that I found quite interesting and appropriate today: "Sociologist, politicians, and others insist on defining us into interest groups, factions, classes, and tribes, the better to control us. Our greatest strength is in the uniqueness of each of us. Everyone has something to contribute, but sociopaths, who have no genuine human feelings other than a lust for power, are great at faking them. Some are street thugs, others are among the elite and privileged groups in society. Some suffer from madness and that potential lies in every heart. Think of Nazi Germany and Auschwitz and Dachau, the slaughter in Cambodia, the tens of millions murdered by Stalin and Mao. When feverish politics and demented ideology entwine, those who are not well anchored to the beliefs that allow a civil society can be swept away, becoming part of the storm of madness that lays waste to everything."

THE THREAT IS REAL AND THE THREAT IS NOW

There is a real threat to our democracy. We have gotten soft and seem to think that the world owes us something rather than having to work and solve our problems. Too many people are living in a world of alternate reality. We have become believers in fantasy and easily succumbed to the propaganda on social media and propagandized news programs. Instead of engaging in actual conversation with each other we text where we can safely say all the nasty things we want that we wouldn't dare say to a person's face. Rather than attempt to learn the facts about a subject we just accept what someone puts on social media and turn around and spread the information whether it is true or not. Radical groups from the left and right take advantage of this to deepen the divisions and promote their own agendas.

There is no such thing as "alternative facts". Facts are facts. But, if you keep telling a lie over and over again, eventually some people start believing it. If you keep telling people that someone else is responsible for their problems they will believe it. If you keep telling people that the only way to solve their problems is through violence, they will commit it. There is no way to fight this but to shine the light of truth on the lies. Even so, there are some people that will still deny the truth because lying is how they gain and maintain power. P.T. Barnum supposedly said, "There is a sucker born every minute" and as any confidence man, charlatan, or crook will tell you, it is true.

President Lincoln warned us as to the threat to our democracy from within:

"All the armies of Europe, Asia, and Africa combined, with all the treasure of the earth (our own excepted) in their military chest; with a Buonaparte for a commander, could not by force, take a drink from the Ohio, or make a track on the Blue Ridge, in a trial of a thousand years. At what point then is the approach of danger to be expected? I answer, **if it ever reach us, it must spring up amongst us. It cannot come from abroad. If destruction be our lot, we must ourselves be its author and finisher. As a nation of freemen, we must live through all time, or die by suicide.**"

Political parties

President Washington was right. Political parties can be dangerous. The Federalist were the first political party formed in 1789 and lasted until 1824. We have had a lot of different political parties promoting some specific agenda, most which faded away or merged into one of the main political parties at the time. Today we have two major parties: Democrat (Modern Liberalism) founded in 1828 with currently 47,106,084 registered members, Republican (Traditional Conservatism) founded in 1854 with currently 35,041,482 registered members. A large number of Americans don't belong to either party.

According to the Federal Election Commission results reported by the states to them for the 2020 Presidential election, the Democrats had 81,268,924 votes, the Republicans 74,216,154 votes. Compare these numbers to those that belong to either party.

We have had groups that have opposed our Constitution and our idea of democracy for years. Many of those groups have at times attempted to take over the political parties. The Klan was one of the most notable in recent history and actually in the early 20th century was quite open about what they wanted and had millions of members and not just in the South. Many politicians actually bent to them for many years or they wouldn't get elected. Southern Democrats (more commonly called Dixiecrats when I was young), were quietly associated with them.

It took the election of Nixon before the Dixiecrats broke away from the Democrats and became Republicans. Selling the idea of the "Silent Majority" and the idea of law and order being restored, it was a deliberate move by the GOP to capture the southern voter. The GOP created an **"Enemy Within"** playing to the fears of the people. They took the anti-war movement and portrayed the protesters as traitors and marijuana smoking druggies. When Black Americans protested against discrimination and demanded their voting rights, they portrayed them as heroin users and Communist wanting to destroy the country and a lot of America bought into it. We wanted order restored.

Meanwhile the people selling us on our "problems" were busy breaking the law and trying to enhance their control and power over our political system. Fortunately once the truth became known as to the illegal activities going on by the Nixon administration. The GOP leaders in congress stepped up and told him it was time to resign and leave. He didn't get impeached and no legal action was taken against him for breaking the law. It set a dangerous precedent. Years later in an interview with David Frost, Nixon was asked why he authorized burglaries, wiretapping, and other illegal activities against people, he said, "When a president does it, it means that it is not illegal." That might hold true for kings, dictators, and other autocrats, but not presidents in a democracy.

There are groups and individuals in our country that believe more in an autocratic government than our Constitutional government. They consider the public good as an impediment to their personal interest such as financial, social, political, and religious believes. They play on our fears and cultural differences. They utilize propaganda messages based on half-truths and lies. I have always feared that these people someday could take over a major party and our freedom could be lost. Both major parties have been the target at some time. I never expected that my lifelong party would be the one to fall victim especially after Nixon.

It used to be that our leaders even though they might disagree on some political objectives would sit down and talk things out. They knew that you aren't always going to get 100% of what you want but maybe by compromising on an issue you might get something for your constituents that they could support.

Members of Congress no matter which party they belong to would get together and socialize, build rapport with those on the other side and maybe find common ground on issues. When Newt Gingrich became Speaker of the House, that's when I saw that something different was going on in our party. Fortunately he eventually lost power because of ethics violation.

I thought we were going to get back on track until along came Mitch McConnell, from my birth state Kentucky, who rose to the position of Senate Majority leader. I felt right away that this was someone who loves having power. While he was majority leader in the Senate, he held a level of national power that few people ever hold and he let everyone know it. Instead of using that position though in a positive way he decided to automatically oppose and obstruct anything the other side proposed. He had his own agenda. That cost the party in the long run. As the leader of the now minority party he has continued to obstruct and when Trump was twice impeached, even though he would say what Trump did was wrong, he wouldn't step up and move the party to do what was right, even after the attack on the Capitol. He wants to be the majority leader again and won't make waves.

Kevin McCarthy in the House is the same way. He has flip-flopped over and over again about Trump because he is scared that if the party wins the House he won't be Speaker of the House. The GOP leadership has decided to put their personal goals ahead of the country. During the 2020 election they didn't even have a platform other than re-elect Trump. They have decided that anyone on the other side is an enemy. They have allowed a quasi-Republican party, MAGA Republicans to take control and hold their allegiance to a person rather than the Constitution. The GOP has turned its back on what the party has always stood for. It is like a disease that has spread down to the state and local levels and is a threat to our democracy.

No one in the Republican Party thought Trump would get the nomination for President and when he did, they definitely didn't think he would win. When he did they fell apart. When he broke the law, they had the power to stop him, but they didn't. Why? Were they really such cowards not to standup for what was right and living up to their oath to the Constitution? Apparently so. What happened to believing in law and order? Is getting re-elected to your position more important than your Constitutional duties and responsibilities and living up to the oath you took? Once again look at the numbers: **According to the Federal Election Commission results reported by the states to them for the 2020 Presidential election, the Democrats had 81,268,924 votes, the Republicans 74,216,154 votes.** Trump lost the popular vote and he lost the Electoral College vote. You know it, I know it, the GOP, and anyone dealing in reality knows it. There was no widespread voter fraud. As a matter of fact in those states where these claims were being made, the election rules were written mostly by the GOP. It was a lie made up by Trump and his cohorts and the Republican Party knows it. **Your allegiance is supposed to be to the Constitution and the American people, not to an individual**. Stop and tell the people the truth. If you were on the ballot and got elected, you know it was a fair election or you wouldn't have been elected, right, or did **you** falsify your election?

I do believe that we have a lot of good people in Congress motivated the same way I was to serve my country in the military. There are members in both parties that sincerely want to do the right things, protect and defend the Constitution, insure our rights to vote, give all Americans an equal chance, and they honor their oath. They want to insure the laws are followed and want to represent the needs and desires of the people that sent them there. Those people deserve our support. They don't deserve having their lives or the lives of their families being threaten. But, we also have people in office and running for office that do undemocratic things like give their loyalty to an individual promoting lies, rather than the

Constitution they swear an oath to. They turn a blind eye to openly violations of the law and Constitution. They support and defend actions that if it was committed by the opposing side they would raise holy hell about. They act as if they want an autocratic government rather than a democracy. Why? Surely it isn't the money. Whether you are a Senator or a Representative your salary is $174,000 a year, plus benefits. Your health insurance is the Affordable Care Act (Obama Care), and your retirement is funded through taxes and participant contributions, but you have to be at least 62 to draw retirement and have served at least 5 years. If you are the Speaker of the House you make $223,500, and if you are the Majority Leader or Minority Leader in either the Senate or House, you make $193,400. By the way the Vice-President, he makes $230,700 plus benefits and the President makes $400,000 plus some outstanding benefits. Senior leaders in corporations make more than that. So what it is it? The only thing I can figure out is the **Power, EGO trip, and what the position might get them later.**

I HAVE SOME SERIOUS CONCERNS:

Voting rights. Protecting your right to vote it is the heart of our democracy. It starts in your hometown and state. Become a **knowledgeable voter**. Do some research on the candidates. Don't just take a political ad or a Facebook posting or a QAnon conspiracy statement as gospel. Don't let your local politicians take away your voting rights with unreasonable requirements to qualify as a voter or nullify your vote by allowing state legislators or secretaries of state, to override the election just because they don't like the results. You can protect your rights by making sure that you, your family, friends, and neighbors get registered to vote and go do it. Push to make voting as easy as possible. Don't let the MAGA-Republicans take away early voting, mail-in voting, or using **secure** voting drop boxes. It was proven in the 2020 election that these methods are safe. Why are they trying to make it more difficult for you to vote? Because they don't believe they can win if you vote.

Support those people that step up and volunteer their time to insure you have a place to vote, and that the voting is accurate and fair. Too many are being threaten and driven off for doing their civic duty. Don't let thugs scare people away from their polling place. If you see it happening, call the police.

Gerrymandering is the process where the political party in power is able to redraw a local voting district map giving their party the advantage is a major problem. The voting district ends up scattered all over the place. Both parties are guilty of this. It is undemocratic. We have got to put an end to the parties being able to do this. A district should be based strictly of the number of people living in the same contingent geographic area. It should not to be based upon the cultural, racial, or party registration. How many live there in that geographic area? That's it. If you can't win the vote fair and square based on your platform then maybe there is something wrong with your platform.

Dark money is another problem. Dark money is funds raised for the purpose of influencing elections by nonprofit organizations that are not required to disclose the identities of their donors. Both parties get it but the MAGA-Republican Party definitely has the biggest hand in it. The Citizens United decision by the Supreme Court gave the green light to corporations, including certain types of nonprofit corporations, to spend money on political ads that expressly called for the election or defeat of federal candidates. A prior U.S. Supreme Court ruling in 2007, allowed corporations, including certain types of nonprofit corporations, to spend money on issue ads during the run-up to elections — so long as they did not overtly call for the election or defeat of candidates. The Bipartisan Reform Act 2002 had banned both types of corporate spending in politics. Now that these restrictions have been overturned, politically active nonprofit groups are spending more money than ever to directly influence elections. Interestingly during the Citizens United decision, 8 justices did agree that disclosure of where the money comes from is important because "transparency allows the electorate to make informed decisions and give proper weight to different speakers and messages". What kind of money are we talking about? How about one person giving $1.6 billion to one of these groups?

As recent as August 22, 2022, Ken Vogel of the New York Times ran the story of a $1.6 billion donation to a GOP Conservative Group run by Leonard A. Leo, by Barie Seid, an electronics manufacturing mogul. Leo help engineer the conservative dominance of the Supreme Court and to **finance battles over abortion rights, voting rules, and climate change policy.** Leo's group is a non-profit called the Marble Freedom Trust. So now we know where at least this money came from, but how about other money? How much dark money maybe comes from someone overseas to influence our elections?

The maximum that you or I can contribute to a candidate's election is $2800 for the primary and $2800 to the general election. Who is going to have the candidate's attention you and me or Leonard Leo? Members of Congress are prohibited from receiving money that appears to influence the way they vote on legislation, however these dark money groups don't give the money to the campaign. They run their own ads and claim that it doesn't support any particular candidate. Right!

I also think it is wrong when the political parties directly interfere in the primaries of the other party. What am I talking about? During the current mid-terms the Democrats were buying ads supporting some MAGA Republicans hoping they would get the nomination for office because they felt it would be easier to defeat them than a mainstream Republican. The result: there were Republicans running for re-election that had supported the passage of bi-partisan legislation and had voted for Trump's impeachment that lost their primaries. What if that MAGA Republican gets elected? Whose fault would it be? This activity isn't anything new and both parties have done this in the past.

Radicalism and armed militias

Radical groups are nothing new. From a political viewpoint both the left and the right have their fair share. What is troubling today in America, if you do some research on them, is that the radicals are expanding their influence and being accepted as "good people" even though they seem to be mainly hate groups which hate anyone who belongs to a different ethnic group, religion, sex, and sexual orientation. These hate groups will use propaganda based on lies and violence to achieve their desires and want to tear down our democracy. I afraid that my old party has fallen into their trap and has deserted the ideals of the real GOP. All you have to do is listen to FOX News and what the MAGA politicians are saying.

We also have armed militias many of which are just dying to start another revolution and are very open about it. We saw some of them January 6 storming the nation's capital. We have seen them on the streets during peaceful demonstrations by citizens and turning to violence against the demonstrators, and we have seen them where we vote trying to intimidate voters and we see the

MAGA Republicans condoning and supporting their actions.

Researching on Wikipedia I found where the Southern Poverty Law Center identified 1020 organized and active hate groups currently operating in the U.S. as of 2019. Their breakout was 51 Ku Klux Klan; 112 neo-Nazi, 148 white nationalist; 63 racist skinheads; 17 Christian identity; 36 neo-Confederate; 264 Black Nationalist; 17 anti-immigrant; 49 anti-LGBT; 100 anti-Muslim; and 163 other hate groups.

Now if that isn't enough to keep you up at night, in 2016 the SPLC also identified 165 armed militia groups (there are groups in every state) and some with a national presence in 2020 included The Constitutional Sheriffs, Oath Keepers, Three Percenters, and the Not Fucking Around Coalition. Any these names sound familiar, maybe from January 6, 2021? Too many of them are being praised by today's MAGA Republicans.

How about Antifa? Had you ever heard of Antifa before the Trump presidency? Probably not, I know I never had, but the name goes all the way back to 1930 Germany as an anti-Fascist movement. **According to the FBI it isn't a unified organization but a movement without a leadership structure and no chain of command.**

Their stated politics and methods are to stop white supremacists, fascists, and neo-Nazis. The majority of their activities are non-violent. According to Mark Bray, author and historian of human rights, terrorism, and politics in modern Europe, at Rutgers University, individuals in the movement tend to hold anti-authoritarian, anti-capitalist, anti-fascist, and anti-state views. A majority are anarchist, communist, and socialist, who describe themselves as revolutionist. They don't conform with the Democrat Party believes, yet the MAGA group likes to point to them as the guilty participants supporting the Democrats even when it is proven that extreme right wing groups physically attack our government.

What's the difference between the radical groups and protest movements? Peaceful demonstration. We all have a right to demonstrate our opposition to what we consider to be an injustice and draw public attention to an issue we support. It is guaranteed in the Constitution. Peaceful is the key word. Breaking windows, setting fires, accosting law enforcement is not peaceful. Follow the law for having a demonstration and don't let radical elements get you sucked into a confrontation.

Racism in America

We need to be honest about the fact that racism does exist in America. It has been here from the very founding of our country. Slavery did exist, and many of the founders of our country were slave holders. Not every white person was a slave holder. There were many whites that opposed slavery but 300 years ago slavery was pretty much acceptable world-wide. History was filled with nations that conquered people and made slaves of them. That doesn't make it acceptable today and discriminating against someone because of their race, religion, or cultural difference is unacceptable.

We fought a civil war in this country and despite the attempts to say it was over states' rights, it was over slavery. The civil war and amendments to the Constitution may have done away with slavery but the discrimination continued. State laws were passed to minimize the rights of minorities and harmful actions were taken against them when they were trying to be successful and exercise their rights as American citizens. This went on all the way into the 20th Century and there are still attempts to do so today. We have a responsibility to oppose these attempts. One way is to shed the light of honest history in our schools. If we don't then history has a way of repeating itself. As an example; my wife was born and educated in Oklahoma. She was never taught anything in school about the Tulsa Race Massacre of the 1920s, when the African American section of Tulsa, known as the "Black Wall Street" of America was burned down and hundreds of Black American citizens were killed by armed whites and even bombed from the air. This kind of stuff happened in other parts of the country also.

I mentioned earlier about Race Relations Training in the Air Force. It was a step in the right direction. It didn't solve all the problems, but it did bring awareness to the force and with that awareness progress was made in how we treated each other. We learned that showing respect to another person no matter what their race or cultural difference, made us a better fighting force. Minorities don't want to take over the country and take away the rights of whites. They just want to have the same rights and opportunities of being an American.

We can't change what happened in the past. We aren't responsible for what our ancestors did or were victims of, but we can come together and make a difference in the present and for the future ensuring it doesn't happen again. If we don't, our democracy may fail.

Law and order

We are a nation of laws. Our democracy depends on it. There can't be one standard for one group and another standard for others. The law has to be equal in the treatment of all citizens. **No one is above the law.**

Most law enforcement officers are good people. They have one of the most dangerous careers you can enter. Sure there are some bad apples in law enforcement just as there is in any career field. We depend on these people and they deserve our support. If you live in a dangerous neighborhood who are you going to call when trouble develops and you need help? That's why the idea of defunding the police is absolutely stupid. What we need is to better fund the police to insure they are better manned, trained, equipped, and supported.

Too many Democrat politicians and minority leaders have been promoting the defunding of law enforcement. The majority of citizens realize the importance of law enforcement. Now that the FBI served a search warrant on Trump, even the

MAGAs are saying to defund the FBI. Defunding is all political hogwash by both sides.

Fiscal responsibility, taxes, and spending

George Washington in his farewell address, warned about the National Debt and how we should try to stay away from debt as a nation. He believed that we should only borrow money in a real emergency and pay that debt off as soon as possible. He stressed the need for federal taxes as that is where the capital comes from to operate the government and support the programs. We haven't been very attentive to his advice. Only one President has ever paid off the national debt and that was President Jackson on January 8, 1835.

Looking at the National Debt Clock, August 30, 2022, our current national debt is almost **$31 trillion dollars** and growing. That's $92,621 per person. Current government revenue is approximately $3.8 trillion per year. **October 2021, the debt was $28.9 trillion with $22.6 trillion of that owed to the public and foreign governments.** You think we might have a problem here?

If you remember from the chapter on Clinton, he had a balanced budget and a surplus which allowed paying off $360 billion of the national debt and it was projected that we would have the debt paid off within a decade. When he left office **the national debt was $5.6 trillion of which $4.5 trillion of that was owed to Social Security.** What happened? Every time the GOP had control, a huge tax break was given to large businesses and the wealthy. We actually have many of the largest corporations being able to avoid paying any taxes, the wealthy paying a lower percentage of income taxes than the lower 50% of the country, and we ended up in a 20 year war in the Mideast and Afghanistan and borrowing the money to pay for the war.

Nothing is free. The federal government doesn't **give** you anything. Taxpayers pay for all our social programs and wars. When the government borrows money we are deeper in debt. When that debt is to foreign countries we are put into a disadvantageous position. What is the solution? You either have to reduce spending which means cutting programs or **increase government income and the only way you can do that is by raising taxes.** Big business and the wealthy have got to pay their fair share or the country will go bankrupt. I am not an economic expert, but the theory of trickle-down economics which has been a mainstay of the Republican economic platform for years, doesn't work. Giving big tax breaks has just resulted in the wealthy getting wealthier. Corporations don't give the employees the benefits of the tax break, but the shareholders and executives make out like bandits. In 1965 a CEO made 20 times a typical worker's pay. It has now jumped to 271 times a typical worker's pay. When the government has made bailouts and given money to the corporations, instead of taking care of their employees they have used the money for buying back stock. It's time for everyone to pay their fair share. Deficit spending to boost the economy is out of control.

Attacking Social Security, Medicare, and Medicaid and wanting to privatize them is not the answer. In an **article written by Kimberly Amadeo, and updated May 30, 2022, Current U.S. Federal Government Spending, How Congress Really Spends Your Money,** she addresses current federal government spending. She reports "Current US government spending is $4.829 trillion. That's the federal budget for fiscal year 2021 covering October 1, 2020 through September 30, 2021." Even though these programs make up almost half of federal spending **they are part of the mandatory spending established by Acts of Congress.** You and I paid into Social Security and Medicare. If the government over the years hadn't tapped those funds for other use, the programs wouldn't be in the projected trouble that we always hear about. The Congress has "borrowed" from the Social Security Trust Fund for years to pay for other federal programs. She also reports, that other **mandatory programs** "that contrary to popular opinion the welfare programs such as food stamps, Unemployment Compensation, Child Nutrition, Child Tax credits, Supplemental Income, and Student Loans, are not the biggest areas of government spending. **Interest payments** on the national debt for the Fiscal Year is about $378 billion and that has to be paid so the government doesn't default on loans and it is one of the fastest growing expenses , and **discretionary spending** which pays for all federal agencies, the largest being the military, is $1.485 trillion."

Folks we are a big country and a big government to operate. The more you ask of the government the more it cost to operate and that means more taxes. Nothing comes free.

Personal freedom and Patriotism

From the founding of our country to today, we Americans value our personal freedom. I know I do. I have a natural fear of big government taking over our lives and I know many Americans feel the same way. There are many problems facing us today and quite often we just can't seem to agree on the answers. When the government tries to direct us to do something we just automatically rebel. Wearing seatbelts was a big issue at one time. Now we seem to have adjusted to the reasoning behind it and accept that it saves lives. What I don't think we will stand for is when our Constitutional rights such as voting is infringed on. You can't give a right to the people and then take it away no matter what that right might be. Even if that right offends your personal religious, political, or social prejudices.

"Sometimes the needs of the many do outweigh the needs of the few." When we had the Covid outbreak there were scientific recommendations, such as wearing a mask, and getting inoculation when available that just upset so many people. How many people wouldn't have died if people followed the guidance given? "**It's my body. You can't tell me what to do with my body**" was the response from some people. Yet many of those same people were telling women, that they couldn't have control over what they do with their body and the Supreme Court and state governments took away their 50 year old right to have an abortion with no caveat for rape, incest, or the birth being dangerous to the woman. We have a serious problem here. No matter what I or you might think about abortion what's next. Will the extremist next push to make illegal inter-racial marriage, same-sex marriage, or the right for minorities to vote? These were laws at one time in many states and could easily come back again. Then what? Will we make unions illegal, child labor laws done away with? Where will it stop?

The media

Don't fall for the trap that the media is the "enemy of the American people". It's an old autocratic trick to stifle the truth. It is just the opposite, that's why it is protected in the Constitution, but you have to know what the truth is and who is telling it. The only way I know to do that is listen to more than just the one outlet that is only going to tell me what I already believe which could be wrong. It is important to try to keep an open mind and listen to more than one source. Learn the difference between a news story and an editorial. A news story is just giving you the facts learned by the reporter. An editorial is the opinion of a person. The problem is too many of us listen to the same editorial news programs all day long. Learn what the other guys are saying and then decide. If I have 10 news sources and 9 of them are telling me that there is an insurrection happening, and I'm watching it, I am going to question the honesty of the one that is telling me that nothing is going on.

Be involved in learning what is happening. I have friends that won't even watch the news. Why I really don't know. An informed electorate will make the right decisions. Be informed.

Patriotism

As a Patriot, whether I agree or disagree with you on all the issues facing us I will defend your right to peacefully disagree and hopefully we can find common ground and work out our differences. Maybe we will just agree to disagree on a subject. No one has a right to threaten us or take away our legal rights. No government Federal or state can violate our Constitutional rights. I owe no allegiance to any political party or individual. I do owe my allegiance to the Constitution and the American people as a whole.

President Dwight D. Eisenhower, September 1966, in the Reader's Digest, wrote, **"Patriotism, a sense of duty and a feeling of obligation are the noblest and most necessary qualities of any democratic system"**.

YOU MIGHT FIND SOME OF THE FOLLOWING BOOKS I READ THAT INSPIRED ME TO WRITE THIS. IT WILL BE INTERESTING AND THOUGHT PROVOKING READING. THESE ARE ALL AVAILABLE ON AMAZON:

The Constitution of the United States of America with all of the Amendments, and the Articles of Confederation, Author: James Madison

How to Read the Constitution and Why, Author: Kim Wehle

The Rise and Fall of the Third Reich, Author: William Shirer

The Mueller Report: The Final Report of the Special Counsel into Donald Trump, Russia, and Collusion, Author: Robert Mueller, as issued by the Department of Justice

On Tyranny, Author: Timothy Snyder

Disinformation – Former Spy Chief Reveals Secret Strategies for Undermining Freedom, Attacking Religion, and Promoting Terrorism, Author: Ion Mihai Pacepa and Prof. Ronald Ryehlak

How Civil Wars Start, Author: Barbara F. Walter

The Pact: Bill Clinton, Newt Gingrich, and the Rivalry the Defined a Generation, Author: Steven M. Gillon

Five Families: The Rise, Decline, and Resurgence of America's Most Powerful Mafia Empires, Author: Selwyn Raab

Thomas Jefferson: The Art of Power, Author: Jon Meacham

A Nation of Wusses, How America's Leaders Lot the Guts to Make Us Great, Author: Ed Rendell

Private Empire: Exxon Mobil and American Power, Author: Steve Coll

The Second Amendment: A Biography, Author: Michel Waldman

The Plot to Hack America: How Putin's Cyberspies and Wiki Leaks Tried to Steal the 2016 Election, Author: Malcom Nance

The Plot to Destroy Democracy: How Putin and His Spies are Undermining America and ...the West, Author: Malcom Nance

Russian Roulette: The Inside Story of Putin's War on America and the Election of Donald Trump. Author: Michael Isikoff and David Corn

The Dangerous Case of Donald Trump: 27 Psychiatrist and Mental Health Experts Assess a President, Author: Dr. Brandy X. Lee

Collusion: Secret Meetings, Dirty Money, and How Russia Helped Donald Trump Win, Author: Luke Harding

Fire and Fury: Inside the Trump White House, Michael Wolf

Devil's Bargain: Steve Bannon, Donald Trump, and the Storming of the Presidency, Author: Joshua Green

Conscience of a Conservative: A Rejection of Destructive Politics and a Return to Principle, Author: former GOP Senator Jeff Flake

Trump Nation: The Art of Being the Donald, Author: Timothy O'Brien

Why the Right Went Wrong: Conservatism – From Goldwater to the Tea Party and Beyond, Author: E. J. Dionne

Let Me Finish, Author: Chris Christie

House of Trump, House of Putin: The Untold Story of Donald Trump and the Russia Mafia, Author: Craig Unger

Fear: Trump in the White House, Author: Bob Woodward

The Making of Donald Trump, Author: David Cay Johnston

A Very Stable Genius, Author: Philip Rucker and Carol Leonnig

Running Against the Devil, Author: Rick Wilson

Too Much and Never Enough, Author: Mary L. Trump

Disloyal: A Memoir: The True Story of the Former Personal Attorney to President Donald Trump, Author: Michael Cohen

Trump's Brain: An FBI Profile of Donald Trump: Predicting Trump's Actions and Presidency, Author: Dr. Decker

Rage, Author: Bob Woodward

Everything Trump Touches Dies: A Republican Strategist Gets Real About the Worst President Ever, Author: Rick Wilson

Hoax: Donald Trump, Fox News, and the Dangerous Distortion of Truth, Author: Brian Stelter

This Is How They Tell Me the World Ends, Author: Nicole Perlrath

The Organized Mind: Thinking Straight in the Age of Information Overload, Author: Daniel J. Levitin

About the Author:

Roger Carter is a retired USAF NCO that served 26 years in the military and is a Gold Star parent. Following his retirement from the military he became a licensed real estate broker, and then went on to become the manager of recruiting for a major DOD contractor hiring hundreds of veterans to work on contracts supporting the US military stateside and overseas including the wars in Iraq and Afghanistan. He would eventually start his own business as a recruiting consultant. He has retired from that.

Roger is a Master Mason and a 32nd degree member of the Scottish Rite. He is a Life Member of the Air Force Sergeants Association, Life Member of the Non-Commissioned Officers Association, Life Member of the VFW Post 9969 and a Member of American Legion Post 73, both in Del City, OK where he founded the Joint Post Color Guard/Honor Guard that provides honors at the funerals of veterans.

He was a Republican all his life until the failure of the second impeachment of Donald Trump at which time he became an Independent voter.

Made in the USA
Las Vegas, NV
26 September 2022

55967315R00197